APPENDIX

[Copies of the following wills are preserved among the manuscript letters to Washington.]

LETTERS TO WASHINGTON

FROM CAPTAIN CHARLES SMITH.

FORT LOUDOUN July y.̇ 30.̇th 1758

SIR/I Received Your favour July y.̇e 25.̇th by M.̇r Campbel's man, the Inclosed I have Sent Down by a Safe Hand, and According to your Directions I have Sent by the bearer Six plates and a dish, I received a Letter y.̇e Date of y.̇e 20.̇th Ins.̇t from the Governor of Virginia wherein he has Informed me that Lord Fairffax and Cap.̇tn Rutherford has Wrote to him, Concerning y.̇e 20 Rangers that was Stationed here which has Given Displeasure To the Inhabitants, But he Say's Let what measures will be taken it Gives Dissatisfaction to one or another, for which he blames Cap.̇tn Rutherford and his Officers Very much, and Say's he Can't See that they are out of their duty at all as they are Paid by the Province, he Immagin's they Can be Orderred To any part for the Good of the Country, & as there Is a Quantity of the Country Stores at Winchester he thinks it Necessary that the Same twenty Shall Continue as a Guard, as it is not In his power to have them Reliev'd by the Millitia or any Other Effective Men, Else he would Freely do it, he has also Wrote To Lord Fairffax & Cap.̇tn Rutherford, and Says he is Informed that the Com-

pany is More out of their duty by being Stationed by Sixes and Sevens at Particular houses, as he Immagine's y.ᵗ no person ought to be Indulged more than another, he Says if Lord Fairffax has Ninety miles of yᵉ Frontiers Diserted, he Immagin's it to be his own Ground, and he may have as many Commissions as he pleases to Raise in his own County, of yᵉ Millitia, but he Immagin's them all to be a Dissatisfyed People, and no Person whatsSoEver Can please them, Cap.ᵗⁿ Rutherford thinks it Necessary to Divide his Company into three parts, and order one of them to make this place their Randisvows, and Constantly Keep rangeing Under the Mountains, and on the Watters of Cape Capon, and To return with what Inteligence they Can Get, In Every Two or three days, which I believe will be Greater Sattisfaction to the men, to have one of their own Officers with them, it will answer the Intent of Guarding yᵉ Stores Near as well as to have them Constantly Garrisoned here, as their Return may be Every two days.

The Governor has Ordered me to Carry on the Well and Close the Buildings, and then to make a Return of what is Next wanting to be done, but has not mentioned one word about money, to Carry on those buildings it is not an Easie matter to Carry on So heavy Buildings without Subsistence, but Still I must be Contented & obey Orders, but Could wish times Better.

Thare is 25 of the Caralinians here & has not one Gun among them & I Dont know in What manner they will Get up to Fort Cumberland I have

Inclosed an Axact Return of all the Spare Arms left here belonging to the Contry — Colo Wood Still Very Bad yet with the Gout & is not able to write, but Begs to be Remember'd to You, as Well as Your Hum Servt.

CH^S SMITH

FROM ROBERT RUTHERFORD, ESQ.

WINCHESTER 31st of July 1758

DEAR SIR

I Recd your kind favour of the 29th in a Large Packet, the other Letters therein Contained, I have given mostly with my own hand, and shall take Particular Care that the remainder be delivered Punctually, also to make known to your friends in gen! how deeply you are Possess'd of Gratitude [1] —

Too Sensible of your Good intentions towards mySelf and Company as well towards the whole of the Distressd frontier Inhabitants, which has been clearly manifested in every of your actions; it was with the greatest reluctancy, that I urged you further on the Subject, as I was truly Conscious that nothing in your Power wou'd be wanting for the Common Good, but when you Consider the Strong incitements I had for so doing, I hope you will be good Enough to Pardon it in me —

I am Sincerely touch'd to find my Doubts of an inglorious Campain, (or an attempt of a Campain)

---

[1] See Washington's letters to Gabriel Jones and to Colonel James Wood, *Writings of Washington*, Ford, vol. ii. pp. 58; 59.

So greatly increased by the Most immoderate delays which Seem to attend it — I fear Our Country has Lavished a Large Sum for Little or no Purpose — in short, there Appears so great an infatuation through-out the whole, that I have realy almost Lost hope of a Person's either gaining Credit or giving Sattisfaction : for even this new man at the Helm, Seems to be already Prepossess'd and Certainly entertains the most inconsistent notion of the Frontiers, that ever enter'd the Mind of Man [1] — I am indeed Oblig'd to Say that it woud give me Real Pleasure to See you injoy your Estate in a Private Capacity; Since I See no other Prospect, than, that, of your noble and greatly Laudable design (in taking on you the Toilsom Post you now hold) at Last Baffled and all your Zealous Efforts Prove fruitless — May the Power infinite direct you for the best and Protect you is the ardent wish of

Dear Sir

your Most obed.^t

Hble Servt

R. RUTHERFORD

---

[1] Washington, as well as all in correspondence with him, appears at this time to have been greatly discouraged over the delay attending the expedition. As the season advanced this feeling increased, until even General Forbes himself despaired of reaching Fort Du Quesne in season. On the 11th of November a council was held at Loyal Hannon, over which the general presided, where it was decided that, on account of the lateness and severity of the season, it would not be expedient to proceed farther during this campaign. Information of the indefensible condition of Fort Du Quesne, brought in camp by three prisoners on the 13th, however, entirely changed their plans. On the 15th of November they set out, opening the road as they went. They arrived on the 25th, to find the fort, of which they took possession, destroyed by fire and deserted by the enemy. Washington, writing on the 28th to Governor Fauquier, says : "The enemy, after letting us get within a day's march of the place, burned the fort, and ran away (by the light of it) at night, going down the Ohio by water, to the number of about 500 men — from our best information."

FROM MAJOR FRANCIS HALKETT.

CAMP AT CARLISLE 2ᵈ August 1758.

DEAR WASHINGTON

I Received your letter, & Returns from Fort Cumberland. — as to my giving you my advice about the covers for your locks, I think you are the properest judge what cane be done at F. Cumberland, being immediately upon the Spot, and we can send you no assistance from hence, as many as can, I would provide, those you cannot, their is no helpe for, their Blankets will always be a great safety to them.[1] —

It is necessary the Troops from Virginia — should have a Brigade Major the same as Pensylvania, and the General expects that you will be provided with one against you join, it is intirely a Provincial affair, & to be of your own appointing, the recommendation General Forbes leaves to you, if it is to be Stewart, he must be as Captain to your Battalion, & Brigade Major, an other Officer must be appointed Captain to the Troop, he already holds two Commissions, both as Captain in your Battalion, & of the light Troop, his having more would be inconvenient. — Major Shippen has ten Shillings pr day extraordinary, allowd him by the Commissioners of Pinsylvania, for being Brigade Major.

---

1 "DEAR HALKET, —. . . It is morally impossible to get at this place covers for our gun-locks ; having nothing but neats hydes to make them of, and an insufficiency of those to answer the purpose — The Commissarys ask 18/ a piece for them. Pray give me your advice on this case. . . . Yours most affectionately, GEO: WASHINGTON."

Make my appology to Captain Stewart for not being able to write to him at this time, he will send his Return of the Troop to me, the same as he did with General Braddock, as he is a distinct Corps, the detachment that he sent down to Lancaster, are all sent to Reastown. —

The General has been much afflicted with the Flux, he still is extreamly weak, but I am in hopes he will soon be able to set out for Reas town.[1]   I am Dear Washington

Your most obedient Servant

and ever well wisher

FRANCIS HALKETT

---

[1] Early in July General Forbes contracted camp dysentery, from the effects of which he never entirely recovered ; but he never lost his characteristic energy and indomitable will. He continued in command of the expedition during the entire campaign, discharging his duties stretched upon a litter slung between two horses. In this condition he performed the perilous journey from Loyal Hannon to Fort Du Quesne. He returned to Philadelphia January 14, 1759, and died in that city March 10. In a letter to Governor Fauquier of November 28, Washington bore testimony to the conduct of this gallant soldier, saying: "General Forbes is very assiduous in getting these matters settled upon a solid basis, and has great merit for the happy issue to which he has brought our affairs, infirm and worn down as he is."

On the site of old Fort Du Quesne stands to-day the rich and prosperous city of Pittsburg. To John Forbes, William Pitt (after whom Forbes named it), and to George Washington, with his Virginians, it is indeed a noble monument.

he knocked down with the Butt of his Gun; and was that Instant Seisd by the third, who wounded him twice on the head with a hanger & cut Slightly across his Face with his Scalping knife, with an Intent to carry off his Scalp; Scully being Very Strong Seisd him & throwd him down on the Other — gave him a Stroke with his Gun, & run off imagining there was more, and Came into Camp, with two wounds in his head, a Scratch with a knife over his face, a wound in his Arm, one in his hand defending his head, one in his Thigh & a wound with a Tomhawk in his Leg which he receivd in Running Off — — M.r Chew & the Indians sent out; believe one of the Indians killed & that the Story is true having seen where Scully had Struggled &c —

Col Bouquet orders me to desire you'll be so good as send out Cap.t Poseys Company to Bridge & Mend Some of the Road leading to this place from Fort Cumberland. I am with respect

    Sir,

      Your most Ob.t h.ble Ser

        ADAM STEPHEN

P. S.

Cap.t Blag mentiond his Forage money to me you only sent him as a Sub.

———

FROM MR. CHRISTOPHER HARDWICK.

      BULLSKIN August 3.d 1758 —

HON.D SIR

Your's of the 13th Ult.o I have Received by M.r Smith, I have done my Endeavours to get you a sat-

isfactory Acc! about the flour, but can get no Other
than what you have already got, but that M! Perkins
received one order from you to the Baker for 200
W! & accordingly Deliver'd it, his Miller also says
that several persons at Different Times came from
you to him for flour & that he Accordingly Deliver'd
it to them not knowing or thinking that there wou'd
be any after Disputes about it, y! Waggoner Brought
fifteen Barrels of Flour from Mill & left it between
the smith's shop & y! Stable, of which I have found
Ten Barrels & Deliver'd them to the Contract. & can
give no Acc! of the other five, — your people are all
in good health, and am Glad to inform you that we
had a very good Rain on Monday last, we have not
had any of any Consequence since the Season in May
last, in the Drought there was a great deal of our
Tob° burnt up, & our Corn suffer'd pritty much, but
we are as well of as our Neighbours, notwithstanding, we reserved our plants, & planted them on Monday and Tuesday last, & do hope, if we have Season-
able Weather that we shall make some Tob°, The
Stray Creatures that were on the Plantation last year
& which I posted are now come back again, & the
mare has got a young Colt, they are troublesome to
me as they were last year, so that I am forced to
hamper the mare, & keep her in an Inclosure to keep
her & her Colts out of Mischief, please to let me
know what I must do with them, 'tis dangerous for
me to keep them as I am sure they were Stolen from
me last year, we have a good harvest I Conclude

imagine it would be a good way to Relieve the Grass Guard [1] to morrow in place of next day, the waggons to come down with new Guard & to return Loaded with the old, which would save a Command for that purpose —

Many of the Boxes are in very bad order and some of the Ball lost by their own acknowledgment

I wrote by almost every opportunity that's gone to Winchester for these 3 weeks past for hair to Stuff our Saddles but could get none, by which many of the horses backs are almost ruin'd, our Jaunt to Rays Town added no less than six to that Number, the whole wou'd soon be hurt without I can remove the cause therefore sent off Serjeant Baltimore and Hensock last night to Winchester for hair and new Scabbards for the Swords which they are in great want off, this I hope you'll approve off as it's absolutely necessary —

If any thing new or Interesting has occurr'd will be vastly oblig'd by your droping me a line — I beg you will offer my Complimt.? to Col.? Byrd & the rest of the Gent.? and believe me ever to be

With the highest Esteem & greatest Deference

My Dear Colonel

Your most Affect.? & mo.? Ob.? Hble Serv.?

ROBERT STEWART

" 1 Good pasturage was an essential feature of encampments, and as well as the horses was most carefully guarded. ;

FROM HENRY PRATHER.

OLD TOWN ~~July~~ ^{August} the 4th 1758.

SIR

Agreable to my Instructions from his Excellency Horatio Sharpe Ime ordered to write to you for an Escort, with Waggons; to take Nineteen Lode of his Majesties stores from this to Fort Cumb^{ld} & I shall Like wise wate here with Eight men to Assist with them up & Shall want Provision sent with the Waggons as we have none but what I borrow

Am with Respect your

Most Obedient Humbel S^t

HENRY PRATHER

FROM CAPTAIN CHARLES SMITH.

FORT LOUDOUN Augt 5th 1758

SIR

I Receiv^d Your Favour by the Indians Which According to Your Orders I have Furnised the Carolinia Detachment with Armes & Ammonition, Your Over Sear & myself went Yesterday to Capt Perkinse's to see if we Could Get any Intelligence of the Remainder Part of Your Flwor which the Miller Informes me that by Your Orders Lestways Bishops that he was to Deliver to Smith the Baker 200, ^{Wt} & to Several Different People besids further he says that Your Waggoner at Different Times, Carryed Large Baggfulls of Flour Down to Your Quarter, I Can Realy Git no Further Sattisfaxtion

Indians, and I know that they have discovered our New Road, which go on pretty well. — To morrow or next Day, The Waggons will be at Edmunds Swamp 32 mile from here, and I hope the worste part of the Route. The rest to L—— H—— will not take 8 days, and I keep all our Carrying horses and Waggons constantly employed in Sending Provisions forward We have 1600 men over the mountains, and Several Partys out, besides one of 100 Men that Set out to morrow.

If the french have received their Reinforcements as I Suspect, They will not fail to Send white men out, and we Shall Soon hear of Some Skirmishes.

The Accounts of Louisburg are very good, and I make no doubt, that the Place is actually or will fall Shortly in our hands.

It Seems that the operations to the Northward are turned upon the defensive, a very bad Circumstance for us, as the Ennemy can Send any Number of Troops this way.

All the Vacancies at Louisburg and at Lake George are immediately filled up.

Cap! Graham is made major to the Highlanders

Beckwith major to the 46

Eyres Lieu! Col. and West major to y.º 55.

Munster — Major to the Royal Amer:

The General is at Shippensburg, and on his way to join us, but is Still So weak that he can not travel very fast.

I hear that your Camp is very Sickly and I think it would be proper to move to another Ground, wher-

ever you find it convenient, without going to far from the Fort.

I am

D.ʳ S.ʳ

> Your most obed.ᵗ
> hble Servant
> H. BOUQUET

Pray my Compliments
to Col. Byrd

P : S : as Soon as the Catawba &.ᶜ join you Let them be forwarded here.   If by chance your Indians had lefft any Stores, Please to Send them to us as we have little or nothing and chieffly no Blanketts to give them

========

FROM WILLIAM RAMSAY, ESQ.

CAMP NEAR RAYS TOWN Aug.ᵗ 19.ᵗʰ 1758

D.ᴿ SIR Your requests obliges me. I hope they are intended to do justice to our injur'd Colony, this I have long wish'd for; We have bled freely, yet are made hewers of Wood & drawers of Water —

Col.º Bouquet is gon ₍this₎ day to view the road up the Mountain. The Gen.ˡ is expected on Tuesday. 'Tis generally tho't, L Hannin will be the ne plus Ultra of our Operations this Campaign. I shall endeavor to inform myself speedily of the several things you mention, tho ; many may be very accurately got from the Philadel.ᵃ Gazette, this I shall take pleasure in & always of Obliging you. The restoration of your health and its continuance, will be among my chief

but all the Branches very thick With crab Trees & White Haws:
12 miles W: as the provision was Near spent the Indians this
Night held a Council in which it was Determined that all Except
my self a Serj.t & five indians should Return.

Wednesday the 16.th We sent Back those that were to Return
& proceeded on our way being only seven in Number: We
came to where a large party of Indians had been ab.t 10 Days a
goe I imagine from the size of their Encampment ab.t 100.
They had Cleared five or six feet Square Very clean & had left
in five pieces of Bark with two or three pipe fulls of Tobacco in
Each piece: It is Ab.t 6 miles from our last Camp to this place
the path But in different Crossing many Ridges & Course Ab.t
N 80 W — N B: the hills End at this place & it is a plain Country
from here to F: D: We here left the Old Trad.g path & went
ab.t 3 miles: N W: then turned: S W: crossed the path & kept a
Course S 70 W till we Were within two miles of: F: D: then went
to the N of W: & came to an Old indian Town on the Ohio Ab.t
1½ m. Above the Fort We had a Very good View up & Down
the River: We saw some Cattle grasing on an Island Down the
River: We hid our selves in a thickett till the indians had con-
jured and painted after Which we Went Down The River Within
¾ of a m: of the F. then turned S. E. & went up on a stony
Ridge where the Chief Warriour took his conjuring Implements
& tyed them ab.t the Necks of three young men indians & told
them they could not be hurt: Round my Neck he Tyed the Otter
Skin in Which the Conj'.g: Implements had been kept & round
the Serj.ts neck he tyed a Bag of Paint that had been kept with
the Implements, he then told us that not one of us could be shot
for those things Would turn the Balls from us — He then made
us Strip ourselves of all our Cloaths Except our Breech Clouts
& mocasons, then shook hands With us & told us to go & fight
like men for nothing could hurt us. The first View had of the
fort was from the Banks of the Ohio but a Great Distance: we
saw one Batteau two Cannoes, there were indians in the latter
fishing. We were there in a pasture fenced in With Trees sett
one on another. We saw by the Tracks that this pasture, the
farthest part of Which is only ab.t ¾ m: from F: D: was much
frequented by indians. from Which I Could make no Great Dis-

covery Except of the Number of tents till Almost sun seting at Which Time I let the Indians know that I wanted them to Accompany me to the top of a Ridge that Run Down in the forks Directly towards the F: but they disliked the proposa[l] & refused as they were in great Expectations of geting a Scalp there — however When they saw that I was Determined to go & had proceeded on towards the place they followed me — from the top of this Ridge I had an extraordinary good View as it was considerably higher than the F & scarce half mile Distant from it, there were fifty or sixty tents pitched on the Ohio ab[t] 100 yards from the Fort & there are several houses on Monongahala. there were Neither Cannoes nor Batteaus in this that I Could perceive, nor Could I discover any New Works ab[t] the fort. I do imagine the men parade in the Fort as I saw them going in at Retreat Beating but from What I Saw I do not judge that they have above 300 Frenchmen, the Indians kept a continual Hooping but I Could not see their Camp unless the Tents I mentioned were pitched for them Which I judge were from the fires & the Appearance of the people at them whom by their looks, noise &c. I imagine to be Indians — I could see no Sign of a Camp or Buildings on the other Side of either of the Rivers — After Dark the Indians got to Singing & Dancing from their noise I judge them to be Ab[t] fifty in Number all which the Cherokees told me were Shawnese. As I have taken a plan of the place & Fort as well as I could upon a Separate paper, I shall make no mention of it here — — — —

This march had we kept the path would have been Ab[t] 12 miles the Course Ab[t] N : 80 W— The Ohio Runs near S : 20 : W : the monongahala at the mouth from Near : E : From the top of this Ridge I moved to another place nearer to the monongahala but could make no further Discovery From this place we went back to the Chief Warriour & after some consultion a greed to return home — upon Which we came ab[t] a mile & Near the Trad[g] path encamped — We heard the Indians singing & Dancing all night — — — — — —

Thursday 17th As soon as Day break we began our march which we continued Very fast till 1 °Clock in Which time we came about 30 miles & overtook our party that was ordered back We

ters of Moment to him & Us & If his Come Away
Wch We Are In hopes he is We desire Youd
Inclos: it back to us — Excuse this Trouble from

Y:^s &c

C & D¹

FROM CAPTAIN CHARLES SMITH.

FORT LOUDOUN Aug: 22. 1758

D^R S<small>IR</small>

I Receiv'd Your Favour Dated the 20th — & have
sent Down Your Inclos'd Letters to Alexandria by
M: Cooper —

You say I Did very Rong in Keeping Govenours
Faiuquars Letter to Governour Sharp so Long, &
then sending it to you I can assure You to my know-
ledg I Never see the Letter but allways takes the
Greatest Care of there Letters, as Well as Yours
Which I Shall Resarve as Part of My Care —

I Receiv^d a Letter From Governour Sharp Dated
the 18th Wherein he Informs me that it is Reported,
as Lewes Burg was given up the 22^d of Last Month
— but with What Foundation he knows not —

it Gives me a Deal of Sattesfaction to here that
You & the Rest of the Gentⁿ Lives so agreable to
Your one tastes, it is more then I can say, for this is
the Dulest Place You ever See,

I hav Wrote to hardewick at Every Oppertunity
to Answer Your Letters, as I am sensibel he ought

---

¹ Carlyle & Dalton.

so to do, I am in Hast, & no more to ad, believe I
am Your

       Friend
          & Very Humbᵉ Servᵗ

                  Chˢ Smith

P. S. Nothing is hapened since Last
Return, & when I send the Papers You shall
have an Exact Accoᵗ of the Whole,

                  C. S.

═══════

FROM COLONEL BOUQUET.

REAS TOWN CAMP 23ᵈ Aug 1758.

DEAR SIR

    The Governors in America have no Comand of
the Troops even of their own Province as soon as
they are joined wᵗʰ any other of his Majestys Forces:
unless they have a Comission from the Commander
in Chief for that Purpose

    I have commanded the Forces at Philada and at
Charles Town, tho' the Governor was Capᵗ General
in his Province, and was intirely independent from
them.

    Governor Sharpe will not expect to have the
Comand as Governor, and as Lieut Col. he can not;
and would not I suppose choose to serve in that
Rank : Therefore you are very Right in keeping it.[1]

    I send Capt. Trent to bring here the Indians wᵗʰ
you.

---

[1] See Ford's *Writings of Washington*, vol. ii. p. 83.

FROM WILLIAM RAMSAY, ESQ.

CAMP NEAR RAYS TOWN Augst. 31ˢᵗ 1758.

Dᴿ SIR

Since my last nothing remarkable hath occurr'd, only an Express by Colº Burd from the Mountains, is suppos'd to be gon to Fort Du Quesne. This may be of very ill consequence indeed, It seems this fellow was for sometime a Prisoner amongst them, & had the character of a great villain, yet was made one of the Pennsylvania Light Horse, & intrusted it seems with affairs of such moment; how imprudᵗ this was, needs no comment. Another sent down to the Genl. is tho't, to be taken.

Amidst this gloom of ill fortune & delays, we have the strongest assurances of Louisburg being ours, that our Fleet ravages the Coast of France & that we may hope some important blow may be struck there, God grant this, for I'm affraid, as I hinted before, Loyal Hannan will be our utmost effort this year. The Genˡ was to leave Shippenburg at yesterday, but I am affraid he neither is, nor will be able to get here this season. I cannot divine why Men born down with age & infirmities & thereby rendered incapable of action, should be imploy'd in affairs of such momᵗ & in a Country that requires robustness to bear fatigue, resolution to execute with celerity this enterprise; especially as we have great reason to suppose, chief part of their force were employ'd to

yet retains, attached to it, an excellent impression in red wax of Colonel Bouquet's seal. It is an indication of the excellent care taken of these manuscripts.

Oppose Genl. Abercrombie, & how dear Genl. Braddock's delays cost us.

I daily hope to be releas'd. from this place; my affairs really call me home, tho; my stay will be short there, for I must soon set out for Williamsburg, where you may probably have some affairs to transact wᶜʰ the greatest care shall be taken of if intrusted to me. Yesterday an old Indian named Capatee, who was sent about three Weeks ago from this place, has been at Loggs Town & some other adjacent ones, & has bro't. with him three Indians of the Six nations, but what they report has not transpir'd. I have nothing further to add, but a tender of any service in the power of Dʳ Sir

Your very H. Servᵗ
Wᴹ Ramsay

FROM COLONEL BOUQUET.

Reas Toun Camp 31ˢᵗ Aug 1758.

Dᴿ Sᴿ

The Officer who commands the Escort you sent wᵗʰ Mr. Hoops having not been near me I did not know till this moment that there was one, and adventured a Letter to you last night by a man going in the night, which I would be very sorry should be intercepted.

The Beeves lost in driving are to be paid by the Crown, upon Certificate that they have been lost, Therefore I beg you will order the commanding officers who escorted them from Winchester, and from Cumberland to give such Certificates.

MOUNT VERNON, Sept. 1st 1758 [1]

DEAR SIR, As soon as I despatched the People upon business, I thought it best to come over here to see whether anything was necessary to have your further advice upon, for indeed the Oftener I come over the more I think it really necessary. For with regard to the Garrett Stairs I am at a loss unless I know whether you intend that for Lodging Apartments for Servts. If not the Stairs may be carried from the left hand room, which you design for Lumber, without making it publick. But if it is for Lodging 6 feet by 12 off from the old Store Room will make a retired Stair, and leave a Closet with the Window of 8 by 12 which if not sufficient you may make a good Room for the same uses above, and leave your Chamber entirely clear. If the Little Stairs (which will be directly opposite to you when you land from the other) will be an Eye-sore you may put a door which will make it uniform. The Landing you know is bad narrow & will be almost filled with Door, so that we shall be glad to know whether you intend only the small Vacancies between them to be Papered, or the part, supposing where ours is stocoid) to be also. I plainly see Mr. Triplett cannot do your work, before the Frost, for what with Poseys and Major Wests work, He has not begun with the underpinning, but shall write to him immediately, and if he dont come shall employ any I can get. He now, and but lately said he could not have time, and that your Carpenters must do the

---

[1] On last sheet of letter commenced at Belvoir.

larthing Work Sir that you know ought to be done before the Frosts — And I am sorry to say you'l find it necessary to repair all your out Houses. But enough of this for fear you should be uneasy. And I will endeavour to direct for the best.

========

FROM JOHN CARLYLE.

ALEXANDRIA Sept 1, 1758

D.ᴿ SIR /

I wrote you about Eight days Ago to the Care of Lu.ᵗ Smith Also Two days Ago Another Letter Inclosing You Several from M.ʳ Patterson, Knight & Jn.ᵒ Alton wch. Suppose You have rec.ᵈ & to which desire to be referr'd, Yours of the 27 Aug.ᵗ Is Now before Me & In answer I have not rec.ᵈ one Letter for You or Myself Since the Last I Sent You Six weeks Ago from M.ʳ R.ᵈ Washington When I doe Shall Send them forward Immediatly I owed M.ʳ Washington A.ᵇᵗ Sixteen p.ᵈˢ & I rec.ᵈ from M.ʳ Meldrum Ab.ᵗ Twenty-five Wch With y.ʳ Money I remitted him In one bill of 93£ by Two Ships of this Fleat I Shall by Sum Oppertunity Write to Mr Lewis If the Goods Comes Up their to Immediatly Send them Over to Eaves Warehouse & to Acquaint Me therewith & I Will Send for them, We have Very little Intercourse With York they may Lay their Twelve Months before an Oppertunity May offer of Your Getting them If A Vessel is Not directed to call for them on purpose had they been Sended At Either Hampton or Norfolk We have

Please inform Doc.ʳ Craik of my Sailing — in case he shoud not have rece.ᵈ my Letters — because he has Commands homewards —

FROM WILLIAM RAMSAY, ESQ.

CAMP NEAR RAYS TOWN, Sept.ʳ 3.ᵈ[1] 1758

DEAR SIR (

Yours of yesterday I have, you ought to have no uneasiness, you are not the cause of any delay, your friends, & even those of ev'ry Core,[2] who know you only by Character, wish for you. I presume you know L.ᵗ Col. Stephens has been under an arrest for some time by S.ʳ John Wildair,[3] Stephens says he is

---

[1] This letter, dated the 3d, is indorsed by Washington "Sept. 13th," although as Ramsay's letter of the 12th appears to follow it, the indorsement is probably incorrect.

[2] Probably intended for "corps."

[3] Sir John St. Clair appears to have been so designated by Mr. Ramsay on account of his tempestuous disposition, which also showed itself in his attitude during the Braddock campaign. The Commissioners from Pennsylvania write of him to the Governor that he "stormed like a lyon rampant," and that he in his accusation that Pennsylvania was retarding the expedition, declared "that he would kill all kinds of cattle, carry away horses, burn houses &c. and that if the French defeated them in consequence of the delays of this Province, he would, with his sword drawn, pass through it, and treat the inhabitants as traitors to his master." In regard to this later quarrel between Colonel Stephen and himself, however, General Forbes writes to Colonel Bouquet, September 23, 1758, " Sir John St. Clair says that if I say he was in the wrong to Colonel Stevens, he will readily acknowledge it. I do not choose meddling, but I think Colonel Stevens might act, and trust to Sir John's acknowledgement." Sir John St. Clair was appointed in October, 1654, Deputy Quarter-Master General of all the forces in America, with rank of Colonel, and arrived in this country on the 10th of January, 1755. Sargent, in his *Braddock's Expedition*, says, " St. Clair remained for a long time in service in America. On the 20th March, 1756, he was made a Lieut. Col. of the 60th ; in Jan., 1758, the local rank of Colonel in America was bestowed on him ; and on Feb. 19th, 1762, he was made a full Colonel. He is said to have dwelt near Tarbet in Argyleshire. At the defeat he was shot through the body, under the right pap, but soon recovered."

right & will not be releasd without a publick justi-
fication, even Lieut Col? Loyd of the Pensylvanias
has taken the Command from the B——ly,[1] this has
mortified him much, & probably may humble his
pride. To morrow Col? Dagworthy marches with his
Tatterdemalions & by report is to advance towards
Fort Du Quesne, & there to throw up a breast work,
or make some place of defence.   The Gen! not yet
come. the 1ˢᵗ insᵗ we had Sixty one Guns fir'd & three
feu de joys for taking Louisburg. I wish Capᵗ Woodward ev'ry success, also Sergᵗ Scott. I shall make
evry remark in my power, but I hope to see you
soon —

            I am Dᵣ Sir Yours Most Affectˡʸ
                                   Wᴹ Ramsay

<hr>

REAS TOWN CAMP 4ᵗʰ September 1758

Dear Sir
    I detained your Express in Expectation of receiv-
ing a Letter from the General which is just come to
hand, he Sets out to day, and orders me to go to our
advanced Post, where there is Some appearance of
an attack, and as soon as their Intrenchmᵗˢ are raised,
and the necessary dispositions made for the Communication I am to return here. It seems by his
Intelligences that the French expects a large body
of Indians from beyond the Lakes, and as it is not
in their Power to keep them long, he judges that

---

1 Bully ?

they could be prevailed upon to make a Push at our Head.

He desires me to inform you that the Militia of Maryland and Governor Sharpe himself will be the 10th at Cumberland, where you will leave no Body who is able to go upon the Expedition. That Militia is to be victualled, and to have some Liquor.

As we have no Accomodation here for your Sick, you will leave them in the Fort, where I shall Send a Surgeon and Medicines, wth furnitures of the General Hospital, Please to let me know their Number; and to order a Sufficient number of Women to attend as Nurses, they will be paid.

I cannot fix the day of your march as it depends on two things out of my Power, the arrival of the General, and a Sufficient Number of Waggons, to Send you from here Provisions, Tools Liquor &c.

I am sensible that your March would be more Expeditious had you only carrying Horses, but we have no Keggs for Pork nor Boxes for the Tools, therefore you must have at least 28 Waggons which will be chosen among the best, They will not make a long line.

Your march will be covered by our advanced Post and 300 of the best Woodsmen, and the Indians who are marched to day under Comand of Lt Col. Dagworthy, and are to be advanced nearer to the fort, Keeping continually Spyes and little Partys about it to give Intelligence of the Enemy's motions: When you are upon your march, I will propose to the General to send 500 men from our Deposite to take Post at the Salt Like, and help you to fortify your Camp.

I hear that the most dangerous Place for an attack upon you would be from Lead Stone Creek, as the Ennemy has boats and would go up Mononghehela, It would therefore not be improper to have that Side reconnoitred before you march by, and as it is at a great distance of the Roads, you would have time to make the necessary dispositions, and prevent a Surprise, the only thing I am in fear of with our new Soldiers.

Here is the Calculation I make for your Ammunition, and Provision 20 Rounds carried by Each man, and 80 in Reserve will require

24 Barrills of Powder in . . .	2 Waggons
53 Boxes of Muskett Balls } Flints . . . . . }	. . 4 do.
Tools	2 do.
Liquor and Salt	2 do.
20,000 ℔ Pork for 4 Weeks . . .	16 do.
Rice	1 do.
42,000 ℔ of flour	210 horses.
50 Heads of Cattle.	

I make the Computation for 1000 Effective, including the Waggoners, Drivers, &c. and I propose 4 Weeks of Pork as I think live Cattle a very precarious thing.

If I have omitted any article, I beg you will let me know it. We are entirely stopped for Want of Waggons, and if it is possible to get any in Virg.ª and Maryland, they would be of infinite service; We have a considerable quantity of forrage on the S.º branches which they could carry to Cumberl.ᵈ [1]

---

1 Edward Shippen, writing on May 28, 1758, from Lancaster, Pa., to his son, Major Joseph Shippen, states that he was " engaged to send off at six o'clock A. M. of Tues-

by Lieu.t King which I hope will Get safe to hand,
if you should want any Particular Necessary's up by
the convoy of waggons I hope you will make free of
writing to me Mentioning the Particulars —

I Emagin you have heard of poor Col.º Spotward
Dying about seven Days ago & old Col.º Russell is
dead.

by all Acco.t there is a worse Prospect of corn &
Tobacco as ever has been in Virginia

I have Inquire'd of Everyone about your mare but
can get no Account of her, it is talkt of by some
People the man you bought her off keeps her in
Possession which I am Desiread not to advertise her
yet, & to send a Private Peson [person] to his house
I intend this Day to Concult with M.rs Sniggers &
see if I can get him to go up, I am informd a Mare
you bough of Cap.t Linsey's son is gone to her old
walks on Spout Run this I shall Inquire into

your Peter is extreamly ill I believe with the
Pleurisy, I have Hired a Dutch Smith for a few
Days, until he gets better

we have got the well 103 Feet Deep, but no like-
lewhood of water yet, I have no more to add, but
D.r S.ir Believe

I am Your Friend & most Obed.t

Hhb.le Serv.t

Ch.s Smith

FROM COLONEL ADAM STEPHEN.

SIR,

Please to send up the mens Cloaths & Bayonets; The Season approaches which requires the Use of Both —

Your men in the Detachment have been greatly harrassed since the first of June; on which we Left Winchester by S[r] John S[t] Clairs Orders — Without any from Gen[l] Forbes, or Col Bouquet, nay contrary to their intention as the Latter informed me; we are all obliged to the Q[r] M[r] Gen[l] for that; as likewise for his particular regard for having us at Work rather [than] any other troop. His fondness in this respect, with his daring to Call us Mutineers; occasion'd a difference betwixt us which at present lies under the determination of Gen[l] Forbes, Upon Whom S[r] John waits, all the Way from Laurel Hill, to give his reasons for his behaviour — The Cloaths belonging to my Company were sent to Fort Cumberland, those of the Other Companies were Left, in store at Raystown — You have no reason to Alter your Opinion of the Rout of the Army. — I can make it Appear that the Virginians have Contributed their Utmost to forward his Majestys Service — I inclose you a Return of the Detachm[t] and am with Respect,

        Sir,

           your most Ob[t] hu[ble] Ser[t]

                ADAM STEPHEN

CAMP ON LOYAL HANNON }
    Sept[r]. 9th 1758   }

They will be at CumberL^d on Teusday night, and a further suply, may be afterwards sent when the General's pleasure is known with regard to your march —

I could have wished to inform you of the Generals arrival here, We looked for him Yesterday, but understood in the Evening that he remained at Fort Loudon on friday Morning, with little probability of his disorder permitting him to march for sever [1] Days —

> I am Sir
> Your most obed^t humble
> Servt HUGH MERCER.

FROM DR. HUGH MERCER.

CAMP AT REAS TOWN 11th Septr. 1758

SIR,

I have sent thirty Packhorses and one Waggon loaded with Flour, amounting to about Seven Thousand W^t; More would have been sent, had horses or Waggons been here ; —

By intelligence from Major Halket I find the General leaves Loudon to day, so that Colonel Bouquet may be expected from the Westward before, the Genl arrives here; And a further suply sent your forces, if their stay at CumberLd makes it necessary —

> I am Sir
> Your most obed^t Servt
> HUGH MERCER

---

[1] The ink in the original of this letter has become so faint that the remainder of the word "several" is entirely obliterated.

FROM JOSEPH CHEW, ESQ.

NEW YORK Sept? 11ᵗʰ 1758

DEAR SIR

I arrived here a few days agoe from New London and still find Cause of Complaint against you having had not a single Line from you for a Very long time. I make many Allowances for the Hurry you must be in and the Place where you are —

I have the Pleasure to inform you that Govʳ Delancey last night Recᵈ An Express from Albany giving him an Accoᵗ of Colº Broadstreets taking Fort Frontinack with all the Vessells on Lake Ontario two of which is Loaded with Furs &c just arrived from Niagara — this is a Glorious stroak. Cuts off all Communication with their Western settlements & Forts & will I hope make the Conquest of Duquesne Easie of which I impatiently Expect to hear —

Inclosed is a news paper to which I must Refer you the Post being just Ready to set out, and my head something out of order having Set up late last night and finished several Bottles to the health of Colº Broadstreet and his Army — our Worthy friend Mʳ Robinson his good Lady and Family are All well and speak of you with great Affection, believe me at all times to be with the greatest truth my Dear sir

Your Affectionate

JOS CHEW

P.S.

Please to give my Love to my Brother, who I hope behaves well /.

Colony on that Service till the first of Jany if the Expedition was not over before that time, this was done, not from any Expectations many of us had that an Attempt would be made, after so many repeated delays, to reduce the Fort at this Season, but as I said before that the blame might not lie at our door, but ~~to~~ _{be charged upon} them who I fear will too justly deserve it. a strange fatality surely governs all our Counsells, what else could occasion such delays, whereby such large Sums have _{been} expended without any Advantage to the Common Cause, and so many brave men perish with cold & sickness who if led to the Enemy would have done their Country Service, I am perplexed and tried with finding out reasons for such unaccountable Conduct, for such it is to me, and shall endeavour to think no more of it, till I see the Event, which I am afraid will not be very favourable, I heartily pity our poor men who must be now very illy provided to stand the Severity of the Season, I wish they were all back, for I really expect nothing from their continuing longer there, that they may _{have} things that are now absolutely necessarily for them, I wish my fears may be groundless and that the Fort may be in our possession before this reaches you, as the taking of it is of the greatest Consequence to this Colony. I heartily pray that the Lord of Hosts will defend & protect You and am

     Dr Sir

        Your very Affect^e Friend

Sept. 13, 1758.   JOHN ROBINSON

FROM LIEUTENANT-COLONEL ADAM STEPHEN.

CAMP ON LOYAL HANNON Sep.ʳ 13ᵗʰ 1758

SIR,

We have fortifyd this place; & taken post ten miles to the westward on Kishiminatos,[1] about forty miles from Fort du Quesne. In obedience to Col Bouquets Commands I wrote you by Serg.ᵗ Boynes to send up the mens Cloathing, but humbly Conceive, that Blanket Coats would suit Better than any that can be got for your Regiment. — You will be so good as to excuse me for not being particular about our Situation & designs; as I cannot depend on your getting Letters that I write — Some of great importance wrote by others; have fallen into the hands of the Enemy I offer my Compliments to the Gentlemen with you and am with respect,

Sir, Your most Ob.ᵗ hb.ᵉ Sᵗ

ADAM STEPHEN

FROM JOHN KIRKPATRICK, ESQ.

ALEXANDRIA 14ᵗʰ Sep.ʳ 1758

MY DEAR COL.º/

I snatch a moment before I take horse, to tell you the pleasure I have received by intercepting Your very kind favour of the 11ᵗʰ directed for Kirkcudbright — and return you my hearty thanks for the trouble

---

1 The name Kiskaminities was by some applied to the Loyal Hannon. Later it has been restricted to the stream between the junction of the Kiskaminities and the Allegheny River and the forks of the Loyal Hannon and the Conemaugh rivers. — J. M. TONER.

I have Imploy'd a man of Skill to Assist me in Doing the stone worke of y.ᵉ Bastiane which I am affraid it will be a very Troublesom undertakeing as all the old work must be Taken away & new Pillars rais'd, you may be sure there is no Soldier here fit for Duty but what is kept constantly at Labour to keep things in Repair —

Now I have wrote to Sam.ˡ Givings for the Brand & markes of your Black Mare, & then will take Every Method, I can to get them. I will Advertise them at Every Publick Place, I can think off —

The Horse that Burris rode Down is a Light bay about 14 Hands high, favours a horse I have seen you have no brand's, only some white hairs Groing on the top of his Neck the Reason of my Stoping him — Burris first told me he was Your's & you Lent him & afterwards Offered him for Sale, hardwick says he Does not know him to be Yours —

Your Peter has mended very Little since my Last but is able to do some small Trifles in the Shop

Hardwick has been a Speaking to me that he is Realy Intended to Leave Your Inploy as soon as his time is up — Your Waggoner John behaves Extreamly ill, & Consults his own Interest more than Yours —

I have got one of your waggons & Neagre [nigger] addam to Drive for the Publick, & some Imploy I get about Town that is when it can be spard from the Quarter —

As there is many of the officers Looses men by Desertion, Writes to me Desireing, to Advertise them at £2 Reward, I must Certainly pay Y.ᵉ Money when any

Soldier Deliver'd to me as a Deserter, & they haveing my Advertisement I take a Receipt for the money
I advance that I know, but I should be vastly oblige
to you for your advice, in Leting me know, how I
Shall be Repaid; as I have sent Advertisem^{ts} to all
Parts of Virg^a & some to North Carrolina this I look
upon to be my Duty when Requir'd for the good
of the publick, I Receive one of the 1st Virg^a Reg^t
Deserter from Lieu^t King's Comm^d of the 10th & 3
belonging to the north Carolinia Detachment (that
Scoundral) Hansley after being pardin'd Deserted
Last night as I am in a Hurry, of writeing an answer
to the Governour's Letter I hope you will Excuse my
not sending you the weekly Returnes, but there is
nothing happened Extraordenory Since my Last only
Receiv^d 4 Deserters, hansley Deserted & one Dead
of the old Reg^t —

it make our Duty Very hard to keep so many Prisoners I think it would be very Advisable to Clap them
to Labour as there is a Nessaity at this time —

Mr Rutherford will have about, 30, or 40, Waggons
Ready to start from this Place of the 22^d Loaded with
Flwor & Forrage, but is at a Loss what to do for a
Guard of Men if you think Proper I can spare the 20
Raingers as far as pierce halls, but must have your
advice in this Case —

I have Inclos'd my Pay Role for the Month of
Augt for Subsistance & Working Pay, conclude-
ing myself as SuperIntendent of the Publick work —
there is David Davis of Colo: Stephen's Comp^n Rich^d

Trotter of Capt Woodwards Comp^y has ˄not Receiv^d any

Subsistence for — 6 Months, Past, I Did not know if it was Advisable or not to Put them in my Pay Roles or not, but have at the bottom — without you spake to Mr Boyd Concerning the men that is Join'd me sence your Departure he will not send whats Due to them —

As Mr Redeford[1] has Aplied to me for a Guard to go _{up} with the Waggons as Lord Farfax denys sending One of the Militia & the teams Lying here at Expence Loaded with forrage I thought its Nessasary for the good of the Service to Send Express to You to know if I am to Send the 20 Rangers that is under my Command as far as Piercealls Or not I beg for an imediate Answer as the Waggons Lyes here upon Expence

The Express from Alexandria has not Return'd as Yet I am Dear Sir

Your Very Humb.^{le} Servt

CH.^S SMITH

FROM PRESLEY THORNTON, ESQ.[2]

MY DEAR COL.^O

To hear of the welfare of my Friend will always give me great Satisfaction, but your kind Letter of

---

1 Rutherford.

2 Colonel Presley Thornton, son of Anthony and Winifred (Presley) Thornton, grandson of Francis and Alice (Savage) Thornton, and great-grandson of William Thornton, of Gloucester and Stafford, represented Northumberland county in the House of Burgesses from 1748 until he was appointed to the Council in 1760. Colonel Thornton was twice married. His second wife was Charlotte Belson, adopted daughter of John Tayloe, of Mount Airy. He died December 8, 1769, in the forty-eighth year of his age, leaving two sons and three daughters, Elizabeth, Peter Presley, Winifred, Presley, and Charlotte. He was a grandson of Peter Presly, from whom, through his mother, Colonel Thornton inherited Northumberland House.

the 8th Sep^t has afforded infinite Pleasure, as in a paragraph of a Letter you some time ago wrote to Col? Tayloe you mention'd my being unmindful of you, by not answering a Letter that you had wrote to me soon after I had the Pleasure of seeing you last, wch I have never received therefore I must believe it has fallen into the Hands of the envious, I shou'd be pleased if I cou'd find out the person, & will endeavor to do it, tho' I am afraid it will be a difficult task.

Your kind wishes for my Happiness deserve my most thankful acknowledgements, mine you have, with unfeigned sincerity, and I am truly concern'd to find that the prospect of yours is so distant. I can only wish & that I will do most ardently that success may attend all your undertakings (& that soon) of wch Happiness must be the consequence.

I wou'd write to you the resolutions of the House of Burgesses but none of them as yet are completed. I am inform'd that the Govr detains Jenkins until they are, that you may be fully advised of them, and my Business obliges me to be absent for a few days, & lest he shou'd be sent off before my return, I shou'd have been wanting in my Friendship to you, if I was not to write, tho' it shou'd be nothing more than to assure you that I am with the greatest Truth

My dear Col?

Your Mo : Aff^t Obed^t Servt

PRESLEY THORNTON.

W^MS BURG
26 Sepr 1758.

FROM THE HON. GOVERNOR FAUQUIER.

W.ˢBURGH Ocᵗ. 7ᵗʰ [mutilated]

Sᴿ./

I recd your Dispatches containing the [mutilated] able Accᵗˢ of the Check we received before Fort du Quesne as forwarded by Lieutᵗ Smith from Fort Loudoun on [mutilated] 2ᵈ instant, and laid them immediately before the House who are still debating, one Day resolving on one Sch [mutilated] the next, on another in Relation to Military affairs [mutilated] that nothing is yet determined upon.

Our Loss is great if we consider the brave Off [mutilated] men who fell, but if we think only of numbers [mutilated] inconsiderable, and can be of no great Consequ [mutilated] for by the Behaviour of your Men they shew they [mutilated] not to be soon daunted: They have acted in the Man [mutilated] that was expected from them, and in wᶜʰ I don't doubt they will continue to act, and so merit, and meet the applause of their Country.[1]

I have ordered the Blankets up to Winchester to be delivered as soon as possible that you may repay

---

1 In the disastrous affair of September 14, in which Major Grant was defeated, the Virginians under Captain Bullitt behaved with great fortitude. Colonel Bouquet, writing to General Amherst, September 17, says, " At last our men yielded, and there remained only a scene of confusion, notwithstanding all the efforts of Major Grant to rally them. They would have been cut to pieces probably had not Captain Bullet of the Virginians, with 100 men, sustained the combat with all their power, until, having lost two-thirds of his men, he was driven to the shore of the river, where he found the poor Major. He urged him to retire, but he said he would not quit the field of battle as long as there was a man who would fight. My heart is broke (said he) I shall never outlive this day."

the General those he furnish'd you with. And have
sent up the blank Commissions you desired, and
dont doubt but you will fill them up according to
merit.

The same Messenger who bro! yours brought also
an acc! of the blowing up a Magazine at Fort Cumberland wch surely was owing to Neglect somewhere;
for I should think it highly improper that every Officer should have free Admission into a Magazine, and
suppose it is some particular Officers Duty, whether
Store keeper or other [mutilated] to go in; and fetch
what is wanted from Magazines [mutilated] this is the
Case at present I think Inquiry ought to [mutilated]
made where the Neglect lay, if it is not a Rule, I think
[mutilated] ht to be made one.¹

[mutilated] ry to give you any additional Trouble,
but must [mutilated] you will give orders, that who-
ever is sent down to [mutilated] wth Expresses may be
furnish'd with Money in advance to proceed on his
Journey, for want of which Davis a Soldier in your
Regiment (I think) who brought the Dispatch to
me, came almost dead having lain three nights in
the Woods Almost without Sustenance. He having no Money, no House would receive him, or supply him wth common necessaries of Life. This can
[mutilated] no hardship on any Body as they are sure
to have it allow'd and repaid.

---

1 Washington replied to this that "Gov! Sharpe, in person, commanded a Garrison
of Militia (from his Province) at Fort Cumberland, when the Magazine was blown up;
and had I believe his Store-keeper included in the blast."

I most sincerely wish you better and speedy Suc-cess, being

w.th great Esteem

Y.^r very Hum Servt

FRAN: FAUQUIER

[mutilated] Davis applyed to Lieu.^t Smith

[mutilated] money and was refused, at least his Desire
was without Effect.

FROM JOSEPH CHEW, ESQ.

DEAR SIR

it is Very hard for me to tell you the Great un-easiness I have Labour'd under since Last Post —
on Accot.^t of the Affair near Fort Duquesne. where it
is said our Troops commanded by Maj.^r Grant where
Repulsed with the Loss of many Virginians amongst
whom I am informed my Poor Brother makes one [1]
— I pray you my Dear Friend to let me know how
that matter was and what Fate my Dear Brother met

---

[1] List of officers killed or missing from the action near Fort Duquesne, September 14, 1758. From *The Shippen Papers.*

Royal Americans.	Lieut. Billings, Lieut. Ryder, Ensign Rhor, Ensign Jenkins.	1st Virginia Reg't.	Major Lewis, Lieut. Baker, Lieut. Campbell, Ensign Allen, Ensign Chew, Ensign Guest.
Highlanders.	Major Grant, Captain Munro, Captain A. Mckenzie, Captain McDonald, Lt. Alex. McKenzie, Lieut. Colin Campbell, Lieut. Wm. McKenzie, Lieut. Rod'k McKenzie, Lieut. Alex. McDonald, Ensign John McDonald.	Marylanders.	Lieut. McCrea.
		2d Battalion of Pennsylvania.	Ensign Haller.

if the Circumstances of it have Come to your knowledge — I have Very Little hopes that he is on this
side death but hope his behavour merrited a Better
Fate. — all his Letters have been full of Expressions
of Gratitude towards you and I flater my self had he
Lived his Actions would have Corresponded with
them — as it is I Pray you to believe my heart overflows with greatfull sentiments in his behalf and that
I am my Dear Sir

Your most obed Servt

Jos Chew

New London Oct! 11th 1758

FROM CAPTAIN CHARLES SMITH.

Fort Loudoun Oct! 12 1758

D^R S^{IR}/

I Receiv^d Yours from Rays Town bareing no Date,
but an Answer to mine of the 18th of Sepr Lieut!
Swearingen with 20 Rangers in Comp^y with Lieut!
Slawter & 20 of the Culpepper Militia is a Guard
to the Waggons as far as Fort Cumberland as there
was no Others to be had.

I have Imploy'd two Very good Masons to Assist
in Underpinning the Bastion which we have Laboured
at this ten days past. I Could not Ingage any Per-
son of Skill for Less than 5^s/p^r Day for Each & finding them Diet —

I have Advertis'd Your two Mares in the Virg^a
Gazite & at Fredricksburgh & Several Other Places
at 20^s/ Each Mention'd Stray'd away On the the
first of June, from Col^o Spotswoods, the Mare You

Your Letter for Winchester I deliver'd Jenkins who sets out this morning yours by M.ʳ Chew will be sent by the first Conveyance for Philadelphia —

Yesterday Orders were issued for the Troops & Artillery to March to morrow so that I flatter myself with the hopes of being with you soon —

Maj.ʳ Wells who is left to Command here promises to take the greatest care in forwarding any Letters that may come up for you after we March —

Speirs & Smith have got a thousand Shirts and engages to supply any q.ᵗʸ of Flannels, half thicks Shoes and Stock.ᵍˢ and thinks they can get you about 200 Blankets in 6 or 7 days but the Blankets they cannot engage for and would be glad to know as soon as possible what q.ᵗʸ of each kind you will want — to whom they will deliver the Goods & how they are to be sent up I have with difficulty prevail'd upon them not to part with any till they hear from you —

Col.º Byrd is inform'd from below that your Regiment is to be kept up and that his will be kept in Pay during the Campaign whatever time it may continue

The Assembly of Pensylvania have voted another hund.ᵈ Thousand Pounds — C W. Steuart is by the Doctor's Advice and the Generals Permission gone to N. York   Col.º Byrd & S.ʳ John has given him an unlimited lea.ᵛᵉ

Col.º Byrd desires his Complemt.ˢ may be made you & that he wrote to Gov.ʳ Fauquier the cause of your not being able to write to him — Mercer is not yet come up — your Cow will come up with us —

Please offer my Complements to our Officers & allow me the pleasure of Subscribing myself with the greatest Esteem —

My Dear Col?

Your most Affec? &

CAMP AT REAS TOWN } most Ob? hble Serv?
Oc? 22? 1758 } ROBERT STEWART

==========

FROM CAPTAIN ROBERT STEWART.

MY DEAR SIR

A Light Horseman was just setting out for Loyal hannan with an Acco? of what things could be pro-cur'd here in a short time for our Men when yours of of the 21ˢᵗ Ins? by M? Grant came to hand upon rec? of it I immediately applied to the General for a Party to Winchester to Escort up the Necessaries but he told me it was impossible — therefore I gave the Returns to Speirs & Smith with Directions to send up what of the things could be immediately got by Cap? Waggener and the rest which is expected in 5 or 6 Days to follow Maj? Wells is to send them up to Stony Creek and the Commanding officer there to forward them — I wrote to Cap? Waggener to give Speirs a List of Necessaries the Men of his Detach-m? may want that they may be sent up at the same time — I have ordered Blue Duffils half thicks & Flannel for the Coats Jackets & Breeches & Leggins and 100 Shirts & 150 Blankets more than in the Returns — As we are just going to March I beg

must be the inevitable consequences of this unaccountable Neglect

I long till I know what you have or can do in that affair I sollicited you for in my last by Miles, as the very thoughts of being a Ranger is insupportable, tho' I am creditably inform'd that these Compys are very beneficial and that some of the Ranging Cap.ts make more money than ever you did by the Reg.t But surely he that wou'd for the sake of money swerve from the Principles of Hon.r does not merit the Title of Officer and for my own part I solemnly Declare I would rather serve in the Ranks than deviate from my Hon.r But as you are perfectly acquainted with my Sentiments, the Circumstances I am under and am fully satisfied with your Inclination towards me will add no more on this Subject —

If the Assembly sits soon I should be extremely glad to get Liberty to go down for a few days and in the meantime I beg leave to Subscribe myself With the most perfect Esteem
   My Dear Col.o
      Your Most Affect.e &
         Most Obliged hble Serv.t
           Robert Stewart

Fort Loudoun Decem 20.th }
      1758 }

FROM DOCTOR JAMES CRAIK.

Winchester Dec.r 20.th 1758

Dear Sir
  We arrived on saturday last after a fatigueing & most severe march — The men & officers both

suffer'd very much from hunger & cold — Many of
our men _{were} obliged to be left at Raes Town & other
places on the road through sickness; numbers of
which, I fear will never see this place — Great numbers are dayly flocking to the Hospital; and what is
still more dreadfull not one medicine to give them
for their relief — I heard when I came down the
Surgⁿ was broke — Yet rather than let brave fellows
suffer — I have despatched an Express to Fridricksburg for some material things; at my own risk —

If the Troops are keept up medecines must be
had for them — Therefore have inclosed a list of the
most necessary Articles, And those will be immediately wanted — for what I sent for; were but few,
& I doubt much if they can be got at Fridricksburg
— As you are present; Remonstrating the hardships the men ly under when sick for want of proper
Accomodations, such as beding, Barley, Oatmeal,
Sugar &c) probably they might be redress'd — We
are very anxious here to know the fate of the Troops,
and who will be Commander. When the Regiment
meets with that irreparable lose, of loseing you — The
very thoughts of this lyes heavy on the whole whenever they think of it — and dread the consequence
of your resigning — I would gladly be advised by
you whether or not you think, I had better continue, if they choose to keep me untill my Medecines
come from England; or whether I had better resign
directly — for I am resolved not to stay in the service when you quit it — The Inhabitants of this
place press me much to settle here — I likewise

would crave your advice whether or not you think I
had better except of their importunities — or settle
in Fairfax where you was so kind as to offer me
your most friendly assistance — I hope you'll pardon my freedom in giving you this trouble — For as
I have experienced so much of your friendship. and
received so much friendly countenance from you —
I cannot help consulting you on this occasion as my
most sincere friend —

I am extremely sorry to hear your bad state of
health remain'd with you when here — However I
flatter myself with the hopes that you are well —
And that as the fatigues of war are now mostly over,
you will recover dayly —

By Mʳ Boyd I have sent down all my Accoᵗˢ that
were not settled, & hope now to clear off all old
scores — If you ⟨don't⟩ expect to be up soon; would beg the
favour of a line from you — I ever am with the
greatest Respect & Sincerity

Dʳ Sir

Your most obliged & obedᵗ humᵗ Servᵗ

JAˢ CRAIK

FROM CAPTAIN JOHN HALL.

LAKE GEO. Dʳ 22ᵈ 1758

DEAR SIR /

this is the 4ᵗʰ Lʳ I have wrote you yᵉ Campⁿ for all
wᶜʰ have not been so happy as to receive one in
return —

I cant accᵗ for the Loss of yʳ favʳ any other way
than by attributᵍ it to Business, wᶜʰ your Warfare

must naturally involve you in — an active mind like yours steadily bent on a glorious pursuit, ought not _{to} be wean'd to a more trifling Attention, yᵗ as to this point I freely absolve you, earnestly hoping, when you have devested yourself of Business, you'l once more look on me in the Numʳ of yʳ Acquaintance.

What may ~~they~~ be the fate of our Arms yᵗ way I know not, but I hope for Success, not more through a Spirit of Patriotism, or the principles of a Soldier, than a Certainty of its throwing an additional Lustre, on the Man I esteem.

I read with infinite regret, the Loss of poor Baker & Campbell, I think the Bullets fly your Way as ours — They seem more to be directed by Envy, than guided by fate —

Its out of my Power to write any news —
& Its none to tell you I am
with sincere Affection
Yʳ moᵗ obᵗ hbl Servᵗ
Jᴺᵒ HALL

PS /
My kind Comˢ Wait on Majʳ Hackett
& Col. Bird to whom I now wri [mutilated]
pardᵒⁿ the freedom of the inclos

FROM CAPTAIN ROBERT STEWART.

Dᴇᴀʀ Sɪʀ

Your affectionate and obliging Letter of the 18ᵗʰ Insᵗ I with infinite pleasure received the very gen-

teel manner in which those fresh marks of your
disinterested Friendship are therein given at once
Demonstrate your refin'd Sentiments of that Celestial
virtue so rarely found genuine in this world and
your steady perseverance in the prosecution of it —
If I know anything of myself I think no distance of
time or place can ever diminish that gratitude with
which my heart overflows for the particular manner
in which you have long been pleas'd to take notice
of me —

About 9 days ago L! Col? Stephens arrived here,
I immediately waited on him, shew'd him your Orders and offer'd to give them up to him as Commanding Officer but he before several Officers said
that as he understood that the Assembly had voted
away the L! Col? he would no further be concern'd
with the Command, only to Sign the Discharges of
the Drafts upon which I retain'd the Command till
yesterday he without giving me the least notice,
order'd the Adjutant to make him a Return of the
Regiment, and that Jenkins might be got ready to
go to Williamsb! — as I knew him, was at no loss to
account for this extraordinary Behaviour, and plainly
saw his Intentions by Signing the Discharges and
Transmitting the Returns was to make it appear to
the Governor and you that he Commanded while I
did the Duty, therefore I desir'd he would either
take the Sole Command or no part of it, the former
he made choice off, as his being reduc'd was not
given out in Orders, and I suppose till then he will be
entitled to his Pay — should be vastly glad to know

from you what is done in that affair and whether he is an officer in your Regiment or not? or if he is what his Rank is?

The Inclos'd came here 2 days ago and as I knew the hand & that it could contain nothing relative to your private affairs I thought it better to open it and see if it was necessary to send an Express with it — if I have done amiss I beg you'll forgive me — my being formerly accustom'd to it in similar cases could alone have induc'd me to use that freedom on this occasion — no Letter came along with it except the Inclos'd for Doc.ʳ Hay; one of the Expresses that went from here proceeded no further than Reas Town where he found the Inclos'd Letters & forwarded those he had for the General by an Express he there met with going to Loyal-hanⁿ

It's whisper'd here that L.ᵗ C. Stephens has receiv'd a Letter from one of the Council intimating the Governor's intention of giving him the Regᵗˢ whenever you Resign — I need not tell you how alarming this is to the Corps but as I did not till Just now know of this opp.ʸ I'm oblig'd to write you in a great hurry but as an Express will set out in a few days with an address from the Officers to you ∧ The fear
will write you more at leisure
of losing you has struck a general Grief & Dejection in both officers and Soldiers the men have already begun to Desert — no doubt Col.ᵒ Stephens has sent you an acco.ᵗ of the Situation of affairs here   I take the Liberty of sending the Inclos'd Advertisements

mencing the necessary preparations for what share Virginia may Judge necessary to bear in the operations of the next Campaign — There are many bad men in the Regiment and it will take a great many good ones to compleat it — the best of our men are greatly dispirited by their want of Clothes — Discontents and Desertion has already begun and how soon they can be effectually suppress'd without removing the cause is hard to determine; these added to the almost insuperable Difficulties of Recruiting and the sad pass that Service is arriv'd at may possibly require the attention of the Legislature to provide an expedient adequate to its exigency — Tents Bill of Arms, Camp Col^{rs} Kettles &C^{a} will be wanted — an Armourer to repair the number of arms that are here out of order would be necessary —

There is no money for Recruiting nor any Contingent Fund. No way of Paying Expresses, Defraying the Expences of Parties Detach'd after Deserters, giving Rewards for apprehending them, horse hire &C^{a} without sending the Acco^{ts} down the Country which greatly clogs and retards the Service — There was no Provision made for supplying the Hospital and Guards with Wood and this Garrison with Water those urgent wants would admit of no delay and I was indispensably oblig'd to hire a Waggon to draw Wood and a Sledge and 2 Horses to draw Water this I hope will meet with your approbation and be paid for by the Country you know the great distance we are now at from Wood and Water and the difficulty of carrying them at this rigorous Season by Naked men —

Some Comp.ʸˢ had very few of the Drafts whose time of Service was limited others a great many of them, mine had by much the largest share of them some Regulation in this affair you may perhaps Judge necessary — Many of the officers have applied for leave to go down the Country for a few weeks to have a little Relaxation from Duty after the great Fatigues they have lately gone thro' and enjoy the Company of their Friends and Relations, But as my Command is so accidental and temporary I thought it would be taking too much upon me to grant their requests tho' they appear'd so reasonable Lieuᵗ Buckner in particular begs to be indulg'd — Be pleas'd to favour me (or the Commanding Officer here) with your Orders on this Head —

You omitted to send up your Orderly Book I fear I shall not be able to collect the Orders from the time you spoke off — Poyne till within these two days has been disabled from writing by a Rheumatism if you think proper to have your Book brought up I will get it done in the best manner I can or if you please to have what of these orders can be got put in a Book by themselves it shall be done —

Last night Lieuᵗ Gist, Sergeant Ostin (who Mʳ Gist got from the Indians) and three men on Furloueh with Liberty to stay at this place only 3 days arriv'd here ₍in 7 days₎ from Pittsburg where Fort Barracks & Store Houses were erected, three Months Provisions laid in and three Months more on the Road — this Fort is 120 feet in the interior Square with four Bastions in each of which they have got a small Mortar Mounted — the Barracks Form the Curtains

and the Bastions are Stockaded — the Duty there is
hard and our Men suffers vastly for want of Clothes
— The Indians informs our people that 150 of the
French went down the River with the Cannon and
350 more (the remainder of the Garrison) went up
to Venango where they now are and from whence
(the Indians add) a Body of Troops will pay our
Garrison a visit whenever the River is open — M.ʳ
Gist says that night before he left Pittsb.ᵍ an Indian
came there to inform them that a Runner had just
arriv'd at the Cuscuskus Town with an acco.ᵗ that a
considerable Body of the Twittwees had Attack'd
a French Settlement near Fort Detroit, Burn't two
small Villages to the Ground and put all their
Inhabitants Men Women and Children to Death
not sparing even one of those that Surrender'd So
formidable a Nation's having heartily imbarked in a
war against the French will probably effect a happy
exchange in that Quarter — and if we improve those
advantages which Heaven has presented us with and
act with proper viguor and Expedition What may
not be done next Campaign?

I'm afraid I have tir'd you with the tedious length
of this Letter which insensibly grew longer than
I intended it — The absence of that immense pleasure of your constant Company and Conversation in
which I have been so long happy and which I dread
I will in a great measure be forever depriv'd off so
sensibly affects me that I cannot refrain from indulg-
ing myself when I write to you — If we must be so
wretched as to loose you I cannot think of remaining
in this Service — That your highest expectations

may be fully answer'd by a change of Life — that
you continue the Darling of a grateful Country for
the many eminent Services you have render'd her,
that you may constantly enjoy new Scenes of Pleasure, Health, Prosperity all the Sweets of a Retired
Life and every requisite that must necessarily concur
in the completion of your Felicity are the most
ardent wishes of him who is with the greatest and
most unalterable Esteem & Regard

My Dear Colonel

Your Most Affectionate & most Obliged Servt

Robert Stewart

Fort Loudoun }
Decem. 31.st 1758 }

P. S. It was unanimously agreed on by all the
Officers that at least a Captain ought to wait on you
with our Address which is the reason of Capt McNeil's
going down to you —

Should not our Address have its fervently wish'd
for effect about which we are under the greatest
uneasiness Col.^o Fitshaugh would be the most agreeable successor his Publick Character exhibits him in
so distinguish'd a Light that he has already attract'd
our attention and in him we believe we should have
some small Reparation for the inexpressible Loss we
should sustain by the Loss of You —

═══════

FROM CAPTAIN ROBERT STEWART

Dear Sir

I had the extreme pleasure of receiving your very
agreeable favour by Mr Boyd and beg leave to pre-

present ambition — But if this or what I sollicited you for cannot possibly be obtain'd, what will you advise me to do? to enter at my time of Life, youngest Lieu^t in His Majesty's Service and spin out the remainder of an unfortunate Life in want and Toils or search for an obscure livelyhood in some private Business — I have not nor wou'd not mention this to any other upon Earth. ——

Six days ago General Forbes left Lancaster on his way to Philadelphia where General Amherst waits his arrival it's said to concert the Plan of operations for next Campaign — when the several Detachments of Highlanders, R Americans and Pensylvanians that are March'd for Pittsb^g arrives there it's Garrison will consist of near 800 Effectives — There's nothing new here — We have lost 8 Men by Desertion — Jenkins goes down with a Letter from the Genl to the Govr I by him send his Hon^r a Return of the Reg^t in which there's little alteration from the last I sent you —— I long to hear from you and ever am with the highest Esteem and most entire regard

My Dear Col?
> Your most Affectionate &
> Most obliged hble Servt
> ROBERT STEWART

FORT LOUDOUN Jan^{ry} 16th }
1759 }

P. S. I leave it to you to mention my having got a Commission in the American Reg^t to the Govr

FROM THE HON. GOVERNOR FAUQUIER.

W^{MS}BURGH Feb. 7th 1759

S^R

Captain Stewart was very sure of succeeding in his Wish, as I shall always have pleasure in gratifying you, in any thing I dare say you will ever ask of me, and in obliging the Gentlemen of the Army. As for the other Affair we will talk of it when we meet I shall have no Objection. Mrs Fauquier and my Son are well and join in Their Compli^{ts}. We all wish you and Mrs Washington as well as you wish each other in which perhaps you are not now on a par. I should be glad Captn Stewart would see the Regiment Station'd as he is second in Command before he leaves it. at least the posts to the Southward.

I am
Y^r Very Hum. Servt
FRAN : FAUQUIER

FROM JOHN KIRKPATRICK, ESQ.

DEAR SIR

I shoud come short of the duty I owe you, if I omitted to cultivate your correspondence by an opportunity now offering from Whitehaven — by w^c I make free to convey my warmest and kindest wishes for Your health and happiness —

Since my return I have been pretty much confin'd thro' the tenderness of my constitution and the

but he made his Escape — with a Guard for his sacred Person, in a most percipitate Manner, consisting of about 60 of his Men — The Remainder were almost cut to Pieces — there were only 60 of the Enemy, and Bullitts Com̄and consisted of 100 Rank & File — but he took Care of 60 of Them — 21 or 22 of the remaining 40 were killed, & tho they were so hotly engaged, Bullitt never returned to the Charge — notwithstanding the most earnest Entreaties of his Men — Thus the Story is told by the two Officers whom Bullitt left in the Scrape — I hope it will turn out better, but I always supposed Bullitt more capable of being com̄anded, than com̄anding — I have thought him brave — but this Tale tells badly —

I am much obliged to M.r & M.rs C—— for their good Wishes, tho I must confess I am not sorry they were disappointed in their Expectations — I can, as Affairs have turned out, and I am safely recovered, offer no ͢other Apology to Them for not being so complaisant as they expected — than as one of the Family had once deceived Me, I thought it was my Turn then to take the Advantage — tho I really cant charge myself with ever promising either of Them that I woud die — therefore they have nothing to object to Me upon the Occasion.

Pray Sir don't think for what I have said concerning them, that my Acknowledgements to you on this Head are less sincere, for I really am obliged to you here, as well as for your Compliments on my late Appointment — You wish Me much, when you desire I may derive as much Honor & Profit, as

Fatigue and Anxiety from my Office. I shall do my utmost that the General may not be deceived in the Confidence he has reposed in me — but no Profit I can make, can equal the Trouble I am obliged to go thro — tis true I coud not be deceived in the Affair, as I well knew the Duty — and I will say 'twas against my Inclination that I entered upon it but I found a Refusal woud disoblige the General &c so I acquiesced, but never did my Mind war more against my Hands, than when I received the Com̄ission — As I have got it tho, I must do the best — I'll take care not to err thro Neglect. Indeed I found if I woud not concern myself that no Part of the Trade woud come to this Colony. and I believe it was in Consequence of some Letters I had taken upon me to write the General concerning the Roads Travelled &c that I was ordered up to have a Conference with him.

If you have Wheat Rye Corn or Oats Cattle, Sheep or Hogs to dispose of there is a Ready & great Market for Them here, and will continue for two or three Weeks — Till We lay in our Winter Stock —

While I was on the S° Branch a Man brought in your grey Horse, and upon my Return here Yesterday waited on Me & offered to swear he was mine, nay even reminded of the Place & Time I bought him, and that I had paid so many Pieces of Money which I took out of my left Pocket with my right Hand for him; indeed I coud scarce persuade him I had Transferred my Right & Title of him to you — I wanted him to take him down, but he woud not,

so I tipped the Fellow a Crown, & shall send him down to your Quarter to Day by a soldier,

Cap.t Waggener is here on his Way to Williamsburg, from whence he expects to return a Field Officer.

If I shoud write you often, & such long Letters, I believe you woud soon desire a Stop to Them, but I have wrote on many Points the next shall be shorter. Even here tho I must add one Line.

[mutilated] beg youl present your Lady with my [mutilated] and assure you as I have often before that I am

   Dear Colonel

     Your Friend & very ‾hble‾ Servant

             G. MERCER

WINCHESTER
Sept.r 16th. 1759

FROM CAPTAIN ROBERT STEWART.

MY DEAR SIR /

A few days ago I with inexpressible pleasure receiv'd your Affectionate & most obliging favour of the 30th. July from Mount Vernon. — I'm sorry that the Noble Profession of Arms, so much rever'd in all Ages, is become the Subject of Ridicule to the most ignorant & foolish Tattlers & newsmongers amongst the Mob; tho' its no small alleviation of the intended Injury that these vain Speculative Arbiters of Military Actions, can neither add to, nor diminish from, their intrinsick value; which will always be

ascrib'd to them by ᵧ^ye knowing & Judicious part of

Mankind, and from them receive the grateful acknow-ledgements & just Tribute due to genuine Merit. — I flatter'd myself that our distance from the Inhab-itants, would have prevented, Bullets Affair from being exhibited amongst them in that Light in which its generally beheld in this Army, where it's talk'd off in such a manner that some of our Officers have refus'd to Rank with him. A Court of Enquiry is soon to sit on it, which most imagine will only be a Prelude to a General Court Martial; I wish to God for his sake & that of the Corps it may turn out very differently from what many think it will —

We have here besides the Artillery, the 1st Batt^n of R. A^s, 656 R & F. of ours, part of our Artificers and the 1st Batt^n of Pen^s are daily expected; and by the great pains the General has taken, his indefati-gable application to Bussiness & constant Regard to the Interest of the Service, we seem to run no risque of wanting, & will be able to maintain a respectable Garrison at this place in the Winter. The Troops here are incessantly employed on the Works, expe-diting which, engages the General's closest attention ; he himself overlooks them every Day (sundays not excepted) almost from Reville to Retreat Beating; and as many Guards are now become unecessary, very few are Mounted, and these Reliev'd but once a week — This Fort, which is yet but in embryo, will when finish'd, be the grandest that has yet been in this new World, but it will require much Time, great perseverance and immense Labour : — The Engineers & indeed almost every body else, are so

extremely Bussie that I cannot for some Time possibly procure a proper Plann of it, but that you may form some Idea of it I Inclose you a Rough Sketch, done with a Pencil & without Rule &c.ª and so soon as I can get a proper one, will do myself the pleasure of Transmitting it to you; it's hoped the three Bastions on the Land side and all the Barracks will be finish'd this year and the rest will be Stockaded till next Spring.

Our Camp at present resembles a Military Colony, where Labour, Industry and Arms, go hand & hand; you can't cast your Eye any where, without seeing, Tradesmen & handicrafts of various kinds at work, and often the same Men alternatively Soldiers & Mechanicks, this hight'ned by a view of three glorious Rivers, and the many Beauties Nature has been so lavish in adorning this place and it's Environs, forms a most delightfull Prospect, terminated by high romantic Mountains, which nearly encircle it! in fine the more I see of this Charming Country, the more I'm enamour'd with it, which leads me to enquire after what Steps have been taken in securing to us, those Lands which poor Capⁿ Gist was to have enter'd for us, I hope the needfull is done, they surely will soon be very valueable. —

The Indians not only of this Voisinage, but of several remote Nations beyond the Lakes, are of the best Disposition towards us, & sincerely inclin'd to enter into & cultivate a strict & permanent Friendship with us, they have already brought us near Fifty of their Captives & Promise to Deliver up the whole at a Grand Treaty to be held here in about three

weeks — We find the Ohio Indians, (compos'd of Scatter'd & Detach'd Parties from different Tribes) to be much more numerous than they ever were thought to be, notwithstanding the great Loss they acknowledge to have sustain'd on our Frontiers, These call'd Delawares, are now eight hundred fight^g men, which is accounted for by their Junction with the little Tribes, that at different Times went from the interior Settlements of our Province; the Shawaneese are likewise more powerfull than we imagin'd, tho' we cannot yet exactly ascertain their Numbers: Both those Nations are greatly incens'd against you, who they call the Great Knife & look on you to be the Author of their greatest misfortunes; the Delawares confess they had 50 of their best Warriors Kill'd and many disabled, the Shawaneese have also had a very considerable Loss, they have between$_\wedge$ just Detach'd 64 Warriors ag^t the Cherokees, which at this Juncture, may be productive of very desirable consequences.   If it is true that the Creeks & Cherokees have enter'd into a League against us I tremble for our Southern Colonies! as from what the Ohio Indians have done, we may easily conceive, what the united Force of such Warlike & Formidable Nations can effect to our Prejudice. — In the mean Time we here enjoy Peace & tranquillity, and the Pen^s ever attentive to Gain & tenatious of their Interest, carry on an extensive and most advantageous Furr Trade with the Savages, conducted under such prudent Regulations, as cannot fail of Success & producing immense Fortunes, so easy a Road to

We both guessed, there had been some Kind of Promise, but agreed that it was right for Me to wait on the Comīssary again next Day as he had directed Me —

Bullitt has wrote Me the Place is to be divided and each of us to have a District; he has already fixed on his, & writes Me for my Approbation of it, tho at the same Time he says, " this I believe you may readily agree to, as I have got an Order entered by the Socioty of the College nigh to that Purpose " — I need write Nothing to convince you of the Modesty of a Man you know so well, yet if youl give Me Leave I'll beg your Patience to read the Proposal he has made Me in his own Words — " &c^a as prior in Application expect for my Department all the Lands from a Line run from the Head of the Potomack, to the Head Spring of the Cheat River thence down the Channel of said River to Pittsburg, including all the Land from said Line & River to the Bound of the Northern Neck, Maryland & Pennsylvania — and on the North Side of the Ohio, to go the Channel of said River down to the Wabash, thence up that, to Lake Erie, including all the Land between said River and New England, then you have all the Land South West of Monongahela to Carolina and on the other side the Wabash, as far as Virg^a extends, this I believe you may readily agree to, as I have got an Order entered by the Socioty of the College, nigh to that Purpose," but by Way of Conclusion farther adds — " In Case the British Plantations are not extended over the Ohio, these are not to be the Bounds of our Division " Now Dear Sir I would beg the Favor

of you to be my Friend on this Occasion, as Bullitt is to be down at the Assembly to direct them what to do, (Kennedy says) no Doubt he will endeavor to get the Affair settled as he thinks proper, indeed he has wrote Me that he expects Me down there for that Purpose. My Business calls Me to Phil^a, it is impossible I can attend, nay coud I, I woud still ask you for this Kindness on my Behalf — The least I think I can expect if the Office is to be divided between Us, that I should have a Vote on the Occasion, as well as Bullitt, for from the Acquaintance I have with that Man, I dont think his Abilities or any Thing else, entitle him to a Superiority over Me, indeed I shoud think myself capable of any Meanness, were I to submit to be under his Direction in any Particular — Stephen is to be down at the Assembly too, not only to direct Them, but also to back Bullitt — he rubs his hands, shrugs his shoulders, and says he knows if Tom gets the Place he will serve a Friend — Tho I was once very easy about this Affair, I cant say now but it woud give Me the greatest Joy imaginable to disappoint these mighty Schemers — they are to have all the best Land on the Ohio &c in Partnership — The Plan has been long concerted, and they already think Themselves absolute Proprietors — tho Ill be crucified if they'll leave the two Men to themselves, if ever they describe its Bounds and Situation by Chain & Compass —

I have wrote Bullitt that he may depend I'll do all I can, to have at least a Refusal of a Place, as well as himself, & that I shoud beg the Favor of my Friend

Washington's Assistance — It woud vex Me much to be disappointed in any Thing I attempted by him & his Friend Stephens. I shall also write the Comissary on this Occasion.

I beg Pardon for using this Freedom with you, and after so much upon my own Affairs, allow Me Sir to assure you, that it will give Me Pleasure to oblige You in every Particular, when my Situation in Life may afford an Opportunity. You may depend upon my utmost Care in executing the orders you have already favored Me with in Regard to your Man, I expect to be called from hence every Hour, and shall return again as soon as possible.

Do you not think it will be proper to put the Council in Mind of our Memorial concerning the Land; I coud wish the Point were settled.

There is a Report here of Montreal being taken by Gen! Johnson with his Indians, it comes from Pittsburg, and as We are told here was brought there by a Mohawk Indian whom Johnson sent with the News to General Stanwix.

My best Compliments wait on M⁛ Washington and I am

      Dear Sir
      Your obliged & obedient hble Servant
                G. MERCER

WINCHESTER
Feb⁛ 17ᵗʰ 1760.

FROM CAPTAIN ROBERT STEWART.

My Dear Sir

With a heart that overflows with Gratitude I
return my most unfeign'd thanks for that fresh mark
of your true Friendship and Noble generosity to me,
so amply evinc'd in your's of the 20th Ult° which I
yesterday had the infinite pleasure of receiving, But
I should never forgive myself if I should by making
use of your uncommon goodness, in the least degree
embarrass, much less cause a material disappointment in the prosecution of your affairs, therefore my
dear Sir let me entreat you not to think of being off
any Bargain or do anything that might cause the
most distant risque of a Bill's returning for I solemnly
declare it would give me much more uneasiness to
be instrumental in occasioning either, than to continue a Sub. for ever — besides there's but a very
small chance for my procuring a Purchase supposing me possessed of never so much Money another
reason is that by a Memorial we have given in to the
Assembly (which is referrd to the next Session) we
have great room to hope that we will when reduc'd
receive Half Pay or an equivalent to it these reasons
added to the strong Attachment I have to this Colony which a number of concurring circumstances
obliges me to Love, has determin'd me to apply
for Leave to Sell out, or, if that can't be obtain'd to
Resign.

The Assembly has voted Twenty thousand Pounds
to support the Reg^t till next Novem — and 300
Men till the following April if the Govenor should

will not have him at such an exorbitant rate, I cannot hear of any other of the Proffession in the Reg.^t
I shall write to Capt McKenzie to enquire for one
amongst the troops at Pittsburg —

We are here to our great surprise inform'd that
the Assembly is to meet on the 19th Ins.^t in consequence of some Intelligence from S.^o Carolina —
Various are our Conjectures — We are all impa-
tience! most are of opinion that the Reg.^t will be
compleated and [a] new one rais'd; should this
affair whatever it may be, cause any considerable
change in our Military Affairs, I hope you will be so
good as to have an Eye towards me, if it should be
judg'd necessary to have a Major of Brigade, surely
my long Services and having acted already in that
Capacity gives me an indubitable right to it, in preference to any other, and much more so to M.^r
Irwine —

Col.^o Byrd writes to the Governor on the Half Pay
Scheme, and from the opinion of the House last Session our hopes are rais'd high and very sanguine,
It would be a vast encouragement for us to have
some Provision made for our future support before
we enter on a new S[c]ene of Dangers and Fatigues
perhaps of the most horrible nature we have ever
encounter'd — Col.^o Byrd has taken upon him to prevent my obeying Orders for Joining the R As for 8
or 10 Days longer, and if it was possible for you in
that Time or a few Days more to inform me what I
may hope or fear from the Half Pay Scheme it
would be of the last Importance to me — I am really
asham'd to be so extremely troublesome to you, but

when you know that my welfare or misery depends on the determination I must make I flatter myself it will appologise for it I ever am with the highest Esteem and invariable Regard

My Dear Colonel
Your most Gratefull &
Most Affect. hble Serv. —
ROBERT STEWART

WINCHESTER May 14th
1760

Be so good as to present my humble respects to your Lady   I hope she is got perfectly recover'd —

=====

FROM MR. CHRISTOPHER HARDWICK.

SIR) BULSKIN May th/18 1760
we are disapinted in sending two Wagings down Magnis Talt has declind coming down & Mr Crafords waginner Refus'd to Carey the two mars [mares] down So that I was fosed to send down nat with them which I Cud very elley Spare I am in hops I shall soon be able to see about my beseness

we have no more people taken with the Small px as yet nor I am in hops shant I have prepared them acording to your orders & the doctors strctions & are all well but the two that had the Small pox & Fortin & Wing & they seame to be very mulch amnded [amended] I beg you will Disspach nat as soon as posable —. I am your most obednt Humble servant

CHRISTOPHER HARDWICK

a moral certainty of their failing, and if they do not
an immense sum will be sunk without deriving any
hon.ʳ or advantage from it —

Another of our Companies Marches to morrow
for ᴧ with the remainder which will not exceed 150 fit
for Duty Camp. Col.ʳˢ Hatchet and Batmen included
we March the Day follow.ᵍ for Pittsb.ᵍ with this
trifling Party which is not a sufficient Guard for our
Col.ʳˢ & Baggage we are to Escort a large Convoy and repair General Bradocks Road — General
Mockton is to be at Carlisle on the 5.ᵗʰ Ins.ᵗ and it's
said he proposes to push the Expedition against
Detroit with great vigour. But I wish his operations may not be obstructed by the Ohio & Lake
Indians for our last acco.ᵗˢ from Pittsb.ᵍ say that an
Indian alarm'd that Garrison with an acco.ᵗ that a
very considerable Force would soon Attack that place
and our Friendly Indians (as they call them) to man
slip'd off without giving Crochan [1] or any other the
least previous notice of it — and a few Days ago an
Express was Kill'd & Scalp'd between Legonier &
Pittsb.ᵍ ——

I shall with great pleasure embrace every opp.ʸ of
transmitting you the earliest and best Intelligence I
can procure of our proceed.ᵍˢ Operations and Intentions and need not inform you how happy I should
be by hearing often from you, I beg you will be so
good as present my most hble respects to your Lady
in the warmest & most obliging manner, that every
requisite may concurr in forming your lasting and

---

[1] Croghan.

mutual Felicity are the most ardent wishes of him who entertains the most entire regard for you & is with unalterable Esteem

My Dear Colonel

Your ever Affect.^e Gratefull & Obliged hble Servant

WINCHESTER ~~May~~ June 3rd } 1760   ROBERT STEWART

FROM THE REV. ANDREW BURNABY.[1]

[A Copy.]

WILLIAMSBURG June 4, 1760.

SIR,

I arrived here yesterday and take the first opportunity of writing to thank you & Mrs Washington for the many civilities I received at Mount Vernon. It gives me some concern when I consider the obligations I am under in Virginia to think how I shall be able to return them: indeed I am afraid it will only be in my power to retain a proper sense of them; which I always shall do.

I have the pleasure to acquaint you that your friends in these parts are all well. They enquire after you, particularly the Govr and Mrs Fauquier,

---

1 The Rev. Andrew Burnaby, A. M., Vicar of Greenwich, was the author of a small publication which appeared in London in 1775, entitled, *Travels Through the Middle Settlements in North America, in the years 1759 and 1760. With Observations upon the State of the Colonies.* His descriptions of the country are quaint and original. In one of his notes he says: " In several parts of Virginia the ancient custom of eating meat at breakfast still continues. At the top of the table, where the lady of the house presides, there is constantly tea and coffee ; but the rest of the table is garnished out with roasted fowls, ham, venison, game and other dainties. Even at Williamsburg, it is the custom to have a plate of cold ham upon the table ; and there is scarcely a Virginian lady who breakfasts without it." Mr. Burnaby appears several times in the course of his travels to have visited at Mount Vernon.

I would by no means desire You to ask a Favour from Gov.ʳ Fauquier because I know how disagreeable it would be to You but if I have a right to that Pay and that I have Imagine is obvious by the above State of the Affairs It cannot be deem'd a favour to procure Justice or to rectify a mistake to which I ascribe this Order therefore I doubt but your good offices will be us'd in obtaining a Countermand to it. When I applied for the Majority I endeavoured to represent the hardship of Major Peachy's having got it and told the Governor that Rank was what I chiefly regarded but that I should do the sole of that fatigueing Duty without Pay when there was two Precedents so clearly in my favour for drawing it I never imagin'd would admit of the least hesitation.

I am extremely uneasy at your long and uncommon silence I have not been favour'd with a Scrape from you since the Date of the Letter you wrote me from Bulskin the Day after parting — I am certain that either your Letters have miscarried or which is infinitely worse the want of Health prevents your writing how happy it would make me to be assured that You and your Family are well for God's sake releive me from my vast uneasie apprehensions on this Head ——

I cannot even guess at where I shall be order'd to this Winter — I beg you will be so good as to present my Respectfull Complemt.ˢ in the warmest and most obliging Terms to Your Lady & the Children

and believe me unalterably to be With the most
sincere & perfect Esteem & Regard
> My Dear Colonel
>> Your Most Affectionate &
>>> Most Obliged Serv.[t]
>>>> ROBERT STEWART.

All the Officers of this little Camp
offer their best Respects particularly
M.[c]Neill & M.[c]Kenzie
Pray excuse inaccuracy &c.[a] being hurried

FROM CAPTAIN ROBERT STEWART.

WINCHESTER 13th Feb.[y] 1761 —

MY DEAR SIR

I arrivd here the 11th Ins.[t] after the most severe
and longest Campaign I ever Serv'd and the excessive pleasure I enjoy by hearing of your welware
[welfare] rises in proportion to the great uneasiness
I from a dread of the reverse was long under, not
only, by the uncommon Secession of your so much
desir'd, till then uninterrupted, & truely valueable
Correspondence, but, my not being able to learn any
thing of you, and tho' I was very sensibly affected
by this misfortune, an unalterable persuasion of your
incapacity (without the clearest reasons) of dropping
a Friendship which I esteem one of the greatest
Blessings of my Life, would not suffer me even to
suppose a possibility of its proceeding from any
other cause, than the miscarriage of one of our Letters, and it is with inexpressibly satisfaction I find

be easily prevented, by appointing a Soldier bred to that Bussiness Armourer to the Regᵗ, and supplying him with a Carriage anvil, Bellows and other necessary Implements, by which means our Arms would be kept in constant good Order, and at much less Expence to the Province. ──

These things may to many appear too trivial to merit the notice of the Legislature, but you well know, that the good of the Service is more frequently obstructed by inattention to the small Details of it, than, by what appears to those unacquainted with its nature to be of the greatest consequence, that the most minute thing in it, becomes, important by viewing it's consequences, and that the neglecting the smallest affairs commonly produce Capital Errors ──

But this Scrible has insensibly become longer than I intended, by setting down things as they occurr'd, without regard to Order or conciseness, knowing that with you, Form or Dress makes no difference — Military Knowledge & approv'd abilities for instiling the most salutary Regimental Regulations uniting with the Senator in you, naturally points you out as the properest person to represent them to that House, which is the Source from which every advantage of that kind, we can reasonably hope for, must originally flow, and allow me my dear Colᵒ to assure you, that, I do not propose these reformations from any vain desire of Interesting myself in things however obvious in themselves may (perhaps with Justice) be deem'd above my Sphere, and would come with greater propriety from

severals in the Corps whose Rank, Genius and knowledge of our Profession gives them a better title to represent them to you in your Publick Character, Zeal for the good of the Service, and a fear of their being omitted by them, alone have prompted me to hint them to you on the foot of that Intimacy that to my inexpressible pleasure has so long subsisted between us and than a continuance of which nothing can more effectually promote his Felicity who ardently wish you everything that can forward and accomplish the completion of yours & ever is with the highest Esteem and most perfect Regard

My Dear Sir

Your most Affectionate &

Most Obliged hble Serv!

ROBERT STEWART

FROM GEORGE BOWDON.

LIVERPOOL 24 March 1761

COL! WASHINGTON

SIR

This I hope will be Convey'd to you by Capt John Marshall in the Snow Virginian, who is again destined into Potomac River by Mes!ˢ Crosbies & Trafford to make farther Interest in the Tobacco Comm. way — and as I shall transact this branch of Business for these Gentlemen, I take this oppertunity in Acquainting you as well as my other Friends, that if you'll be kind enough to favour Capt Marshall with a few Hheads of your Tobacco's upon Tryal perticu-

heard before this that Col: Thornton is appointed of the Council. He had a promise of it some time ᵃᵍᵒ which I believe I informed you of. L.ᵈ Halifax is appointed to Ireland. L.ᵈ Sandys to the board of Trade. What alteration this may make in the Colony Affairs, I will not pretend to say: though I should think not a deal: Any more than the Other Ministerial Changes, and Lord Bates being at the head of the Ministry, – – – I shall hope to hear soon from you, and if you should send me an Acc.ᵗ of the Well, desire you will send duplicates of the letter. I desire you will make my best Compliments to M.ʳˢ Washington, and all my friends you may fall in with, and believe me to be, dear Sir,

> Your most Obliged most Obedient
> and Most humble servant
> AND.ᵂ BURNABY.

P. S.
I have wrote in a very Slovenly way
to you being under an Engagement to
go out, but hope you will be good
enough to Excuse it.

———

FROM CAPTAIN ROBERT STEWART.

CAMP NEAR STAUNTON June 10.ᵗʰ 1761

MY DEAR SIR,

I had the extreme pleasure to receive your most affectionate Letter containing the Joyous acco.ᵗ of the

---

ebbing and flowing well, and is situated in a plain, flat country, not contiguous to any mountain or running water." — Burnaby's *Travels in Virginia.*

Election[1] than the pleasing circumstances of which nothing could have afforded more solid satisfaction Two days preceed^g the 18th the Adjutant applied to me for leave to return to Winchester which I absolutely refus'd, however in about 20 hours an Express brought me a positive Order for his immediate return poor Price (tho under previous Recruiting Orders) was Order'd to Join me forthwith, the Day after his Junction I was by an Express from Col? Byrd directed to send a carefull Officer to James River and gladly embrac'd that opp? of sending Price down. You may be sure that Broughton shall not suffer by his Zeal for your Interest ———

After a tedious and disagreeable March of 23 Days I arriv'd here where I found Col? Byrd to whom I gave a full State of our Regimental Affairs whilst in Quarters, our L? Col? [2] lately Join'd us and to my great surprize he and Hughes are of the Col^{os} Family. Want of Provisions and Forrage detain'd us here these 12 Days and tho' I can't learn that there is much of the former nor any of the latter procur'd We March tomorrow morning for the Advance Post and after our Invalids are Discharg'd I believe our R & File will not exceed 700 including Batmen & Camp Col? Men this you'll say is a small number for the execution of our intended Operations If I may be allow'd to form any Judgement of our Affairs in this Quarter it is that our Fate will

---

[1] A copy of the poll taken at the election of burgesses in Frederick County, May 18, 1761, prepared by Thomas Wood, one of the poll-takers, shows that Washington received 505 votes, Colonel George Mercer 400, Colonel Adam Stephen 294, Mr. Robert Rutherford 1, Colonel John Hite 1, and Henry Brinker 1.

[2] Adam Stephen.

FROM CAPTAIN ROBERT STEWART.

CAMP AT STALNAKER'S ON HOLSTEIN RIVER 20th July 1761 —

MY DEAR COL?

Two days after the Date of my last. we March'd from Fort Chiswell (where Stephen, Woodward & their Comp^{ys} remain) and after a March of six Days we Joind Maj^r Lewis at this place where I understand a Post is to be Built —

On the 16th two runners from the little Carpenter came into Camp, the Day following himself with 42 of his Friends Encampt about $^1/_2$ a mile without our advanc'd Sentries, on the 18th he, Willynawa,[1] the Swallow's Nephew & 5 others of some distinction waited on Col? Byrd and deliver'd a Talk a Copy of it as well as I can recollect you have Inclos'd. I think the Carp^n shews some address in forming (by his Intelligence) an union of all the Savage Nations against us to deter us from leaving our own Fronteers, and the French Governor refin'd Policy in discouraging the Cherokees from carrying on the War from which the French can derive no essential advantage and may in Time terminate in the destruction of their Southern Settlements as being the surest method by which we can put an end to the Indian War — a Fever which has confin'd me some Days to my Tent prevented my hearing Col? Byrd's answer, but I learn he was very concise, gave them to understand that nothing but their making Peace with Col? Grant could prevent their destruction to accelerate $_{\wedge}$he^{wch} (Col? Byrd)

---

1 Willianawaugh of Tohoe.

was Marching into their Nation, and as they valued their preservation seriously to prosecute the means of procuring Peace.[1]

We yet know nothing of the Num.^{rs} or Situation of the N. Carolina Troops, or whether they are to Join us — We hear that all our Recruiting Parties are got to Reed Creek with only fifty eight recruits.

We have twelve Officers, a number of the non Commission'd and near a hundred private out of the 8 Comp.^{ys} here ill with a Fever which seems to be Epedemick and it's fear'd will go thro' the whole we have not yet got near the num.^{r} of Carriages or horses necessary to carry us on, nor one Grain of Forrage, our next Post is to be a Big Island and our last at Broad River forty Miles from the Imperial City of Chota. But how our small numbers are to make Roads, Construct Posts, furnish Escortes &c.^{a} &c.^{a} for so great a distance & with the trivial remains Conquer a formidable Nation is to me quite a Mystery! But the will of the Great be done —

It is with great difficulty I am able to write being excessively out of order which obliges me to conclude by begging you'll forgive the incoherency of the above Scrawl, that you'll be so good as to offer my Respectfull and obliging Complem.^{ts} to your Lady & believe [me] ever to be With the most perfect Esteem & unalterable Regard

My Dear Sir
Your Most affect.^{e} &
Most Obliged hble Servt
ROBERT STEWART

---

1 Attakulla-kulla repaired immediately to Colonel Grant at Fort Prince George and

FROM CAPTAIN ROBERT STEWART.

PHILADELPHIA Sep.[t] 17th 1761 —

My Dear Sir

I arrived here last Saturday in Comp.[y] with Doctor Stuart who laid a State of your case before Doctor Macleane and now send you their opinions But as the changes to which your Disorder are Subject and the distance of Time and Place may probably in some measure destroy the efficacy of what they prescribe I would earnestly beg leave to recommend your coming here as soon as the circumstances of your affairs can possibly permit for when I consider the advantages you must derive from being under the immediate care of the most eminent and universally acknowledg'd ablest Physician on the Continent in a place where you could enjoy variety of agreeable Comp.[y] &c.[a] as well as from change of air I cannot help again repeating my entreaties of your loosing none of that valueable Time requisite to re-establish your Health with which no Business however important ought to be put in competition —

This place is at present very barren of News, this Days Paper which I enclose you contains what little there is except a Report of a Peace which it's hop'd will turn out groundless,[1] — nothing as yet has trans-

---

sued for peace. Colonel Grant furnished him with a guard to Charlestown, where the Cherokee monarch in a speech of great pathos presented the sufferings and destruction of their nation, and asked that peace be granted them. His request was not refused, and the war against the Cherokees thus ended.

1 " No other news stirring, than that everybody thinks we are at the eve of peace. All Canada, and the country down as far as Louisiana, but not Louisiana itself, to be ceded to the English, as also Minorca, and we are to release Gaudaloupe, and all other conquests, to the French." — Edward Shippen to Colonel Burd, October 3, 1761, *Shippen Papers.*

pired with regard to the destination of the Troops
Encampt on Staten Island but a man of war is daily
expected from England with Despatches for the
General —

I have applied to General Monckton for leave to
attend him as a Volunteer on the intended Expedition (in case our Governor will agree to it) I have
likewise requested his Interest to procure me the
Purchass of a Comp.ʸ and in the event of my Success will give you the earliest Intelligence of it — I
propose to set out for Camp in a few Days from
whence I will do myself the pleasure to write you
whatever I can pick up that may merit your notice —
I am extremely anxtious to know how you do and
were it not that writing may be disagreeable in your
present situation I would beg a line if ever so short
by every opp.ʸ for this place Directed to the Care of
Mess.ʳˢ Macleane & Stuart for I'm persuaded you will
not hesitate to believe that nothing could make me
so happy as an acco.ᵗ of your perfect Recovery which
I with all my Soul most ardently wish — Please offer
my Respectfull Complemt.ˢ to your Lady

I ever am with the most perfect & unalterable
Regard

My Dear Colonel
Your most Affectionat &
Most Obliged hble Serv.ᵗ
ROBERT STEWART

FROM THE REVEREND ANDREW BURNABY.

ASFORDBY NEAR } LEICESTERSHIRE, Dec: 16ᵗʰ 1761
MELTON-MOWBRAY }

DEAR SIR,

I received the favour of your letter dated the 27ᵗʰ of July, some time ago; which would have given me much greater pleasure had it brought me a better account of your health; I hope however you are perfectly recovered, and that if you come to England, which I can assure Dear Sir would be greatly to my wish, it will be upon some much better Errand than ill health. - - - I am much obliged to you for the Account you give me of the Cavern; I think it very curious, and long to have the other particulars of it. - - - Since I wrote last to you, we have had many alterations in these parts. The Kings Marriage, Coronation, and Mʳ Pitts resignation you have doubtless been informed of. This last, it is thought, will be attended with great consequences. The City seems to lament the loss of him, and probably will be backward in subscribing to the Supplies. The Spaniards are making prodigious preparations, but still profess great friendship for us; However we are guarding agˢᵗ them. Lord Bristol, it is said, is recalled from Madrid; and Lord Tyrawley going in his stead. The Ministry here is still unsettled. The French talk high of invading us; They are manning all their fleets; but we think it is impossible to Escape us. The Nation seems to regret that we suffered Bussy to come to England; Every thing is laid to his Charge; It is thought even that the French

had no intention of making peace; and only sent him to make divisions amongst us; He is said to have negociated a loan during his stay here for the French King, and to have made a great fortune himself in the funds. Whether this is true or not, I will not pretend to say: It is certain he is one of the Cleverest, most artfull Men in Europe; but yet he was watched so strictly, that one would think it impossible he could do so much mischief in so short a time. - - - Our Armies in Germany are going into Winter quarters; Nothing decisive has been struck in that Quarter. I don't know whether you ever saw Lord Downs [1] Character who was unfortunately killed there the last Campaign; It is rekoned so just, and is at the same time so fine, that I shall make no Apology for giving it you whether you have or not.

The Writer speaking of our surprising the French Camp near the Convent of Campen, Says; —

" On this Occasion the English Nation regretted " the loss of one of its most shining ornaments in the "death of Lord Down, who whilest his gratefull " Sovereign was destining him to higher honours, " received a Mortal Wound in this battle. He was a " person of free and pleasurable life; but of an Excel- " lent understanding, amiable manners, and the most "intrepid Courage. In the beginning of this War " he had a considerable Share in rousing a Martial " Spirit amongst the young people of rank in Eng-

---

[1] Henry Pleydell, Lord Downe, born April 8, 1727, commanded the 25th regiment of foot at the battle of Campen, near Wesel, October 16, 1760, where he received a wound from which he died the following December.

" land, And having long showed them by a gallant
" Example how to fight, he at last by a Melancholy
" one, shewed them how to dye for their Country." —

I am much Obliged to you and Mʳˢ Washington
for your partiality and good wishes for me, I desire
you will both accept of my unfeigned thanks and ₍most₎ sincere respects; and believe me to be, what I really
am, dear Sir,

Your most faithfull and Obedᵗ Servant
ANDᵂ BURNABY —

FROM MR. J. DAVENPORT.[1]

Sᴿ I Received yours By Giles and ₍do not₎ hesitate a moment to Say I Gladly Embrace the offer of going to
york for I like the Description of the plantation in
every particular but that of the Marshes & that does
not amount to $\frac{1}{100}$ of an objection and as to the part
of the Country I am Very fond of because I of Late
Seem determed to marry and there I immagine I
may probably meet with Some Girl that may make
an agreeable Wife and in the Back woods there is
Very few (of my Rank) that I think I Could live with
at any Rate — — — —

I Could not Sell the foder at any Rate. I got the
tops and Cheif of Blades at the uper place and all
at the Lower one is Lost by the frost to about 7 or 8
thousand C [obliterated] hills my hemp I have Roted
all that grew at the uper place to about two acres and

---

1 A miller for many years employed by Washington as overseer.

that Lies at the water Side & will be put in to day and By than that comes out Shall get that up from the other place and as I have made another pond I can put it all in at once I have found by Experience that your Observations on the Roting hemp are Very Just. only mine Stays in Longer I have Sent you down two parcels the course is of the Smallest Sort that Grew about the house was in the water 7 or 8 days the other is of that that grew near McCarmicks was in 8¹/₂ Days I have Broke about 100 ℔ by way of Trial and if we donot mend upon practice it will be Very Tedious the best hands not Breaking above 10ᶫᵇ a day— The Tobaco you may depend I will Send down as Soon as possible Connell will be down next week I expect ₍wᵗʰ the flour₎ and the Next Trip Shall be the To-baco or Sooner If I can get another waggon

I have a Little Corn bit by the frost

am Sʳ yʳ Very Hbl. Serᵗ Jo Davenport

P. S. Colᵒ fairfax and I had Some talk about his placees in frederick. but did not agree. he left it to me to See whether I Could not better myself. and if not agreed to Leave it to you to Settle the Lay. But I prefer this place if it is to be had. and if it is Not perhaps I may Get the Colᵒˢ afterwards. & if I do not I Shall not much regard the disappointment

J D

I have thrashed about 50 Bushels of wheat Since you was up and Doubt it will not turn out So well as I Expected

The cow that was Left by the way was Left at old dods. and is one of the Best in the Stock. therefore I Should Suppose not fit Swap.

however if you think fit Send word by Connell and I will fetch her up immediately

---

FROM CAPTAIN ROBERT STEWART.

MY DEAR SIR

Soon after our last very mortifying Parting I was attack'd with a Rheumatism which confind me till some Time after I had the infinite pleasure to hear of your being so much recover'd as to be in condition to return home — So soon as I got able to ride I went to Petersburgh where I put myself under the Direction of Doctor Jamison from whose skill I deriv'd considerable advantage and on the sitting of the last Assembly I returned to Williamsburgh where I had the further great satisfaction to hear of your being almost well —

You would no doubt have heard of the Proceedings of the last Assembly with regard to the Corps,[1]

---

[1] An Act for giving Recompense to the Officers of the Virginia Regiment. — " Whereas the regiment in the service of this Colony will shortly be disbanded, and the officers thereof, by their bravery, and the hardships they have undergone, have recommended themselves to their country, and therefore called on this general assembly for some recompense in consideration thereof, which deserves the attention of the publick, although it cannot in the present circumstances of the colony be proportioned to their merit, or the inclination of this assembly, Be it therefore enacted, by the Lieutenant-Governour, Council, and Burgesses, of this present General Assembly, and it is hereby enacted, by the authority of the same, that as soon as the said regiment shall be disbanded, John Robinson, Esquire, treasurer of this colony, or the treasurer for the time being, appointed by or pursuant to an act of assembly, shall out of the money now remaining in his hands, or that shall hereafter come into the treasury, arising from bills of exchange drawn or to be drawn in pursuance of an act

but tho' it was vastly short of our expectations yet we had the great satisfaction to see the most eminent Men in the Country warmly espoused our Cause which we esteem a propitious Omen that portends better Success in the next effort our Friends may exert in our Favour — we miss'd your Friendly Offices excessively — I would fain have applied for Liberty to have return'd to Camp by the way of Mount Vernon but as I was by various and unforeseen accidents detain'd from the Regiment much longer than I expected I could not with any Grace ask it — whenever we go to the right about which in all probability will happen in about two Months nothing shall rob me of the Happiness I promise myself from seeing you perfectly recover'd at your own House — I am this far in my way to Join the Regiment from whence I will do myself the pleasure to write you more fully —

That Heaven may Bless you with the Re-establishm! of perfect good Health and confer on you every thing else that can contribute to compleat your Felicity are the most fervent wishes of him who ever

---

of assembly made in the last year of the reign of his late majesty king George the second, entitled, An act for appointing persons to receive the money granted or to be granted by the parliament of Great-Britain to his majesty for the use of this colony, pay to the several commissioned officers of the said regiment hereafter named, that is to say, the honourable colonel William Byrd, lieutenant-colonel Adam Stephen, major Andrew Lewis, captains Robert Stewart, John McNeil, Henry Woodward, Robert McKenzie, Thomas Bullet, John Blagg, Nathaniel Gist, Mordecai Buckner, captain-lieutenant William Dangerfield, lieutenants William Fleming, Leonard Price, Charles Smith, George Woodon, Jethro Sumner, John Lawson, William Woodford, Joseph Fent, John Sallard, Thomas Gist, Alexander Boyd, William Hughes, David Kennedy, Robert Johnson, Walter Cunningham, William Cocke, Alexander Menzie, Larkin Chew, Reuben Vass, and John Cameron, ensigns Henry Timberlake, Philip Love, John Sears, Burton Lucas, David Long, Alexander McLangham, George McNight, and Surgeon John Stewart, one full year's pay, over and above what shall be due to them until the disbanding the said Regiment."— HENING.

hopes that the efficacy of their Waters will effectually readicate my Rheumatism & reestablish my
Health I propose to stay three or four weeks at the
Springs & will then proceed to Winchester on my
way to Mount Vernon and as I can by no means
think of leaving this Country without enjoy[g] the
happiness of your Comp[y] for a few Days I would be
much oblig'd by your sending me a Line to the next
Winchester Court, informing me whether it is most
probable I should find you at Home or at Williamsburgh about the latter end of April —

We have just receiv'd acco[ts] from Phil[a] that Sir
Jeffry Amherst has made a requisition of a considerable Body of Troops (or rather Men) from all the
different Colonies, if this should be true our Assembly
will undoubtedly be call'd, and something may occur
that will cause a material change in Affairs — I would
gladly avail myself of any Expedient that could extricate me out of the very mortifying alternative of Joining The Royal Americans as a Sub : or quiting the
Service — should a Body of Men be rais'd I imagine
it would be no very difficult matter to get me Intro-
duc'd into pretty high Rank, for I cannot think that
Col[o] Byrd will Serve again, Step[n] makes sure of a
Comp[y] in the Service and Col[o] Lewis has repeatedly
declar'd that he never will Serve unless a permanent
Provision is made for him, under these circumstances the great object of my endeavours must be
to prevent M[r] Peachy's getting Superior Rank which
for reasons that will instantly occurr to you I could
not Submit to — Whatever may cast up I'm well
assur'd that you will have a Friendly Eye towards

me — The Speaker who possesses a real regard for you would I conceive be the most certain Channel, for by a proper exertion of his Interest which is very prevailing at the Palace, any reasonable point might be carried. Should you not be at the Assembly yourself may I beg your _{writing} by a certain opp.ʸ to him on this Subject ——

There is nothing here new or entertaining — I most ardently wish you every thing that make you supremely happy and ever am with the most exalted and unalterable Esteem

> My Dear Sir
>> Your most Affect.ᵉ &
>>> Most Obliged hble Servᵗ

STAUNTON March 19.ᵗʰ 1762 —}   ROBERT STEWART

I Beg my most Respectfull and obliging Complemtˢ to M.ʳˢ Washington —

FROM CAPTAIN ROBERT STEWART.

CAMP AT STANSTID Novem.ʳ 15.ᵗʰ 1762

MY DEAR SIR

Since parting with you I have view'd the Plan I laid before you with the closest attention, and the reasons for attempting the execution of it are so vastly corroborated by your approbation, that I am stimulated with the keenest fervour to essay the Success of the first essential step, previously necessary to my appearing at Head Quarters — In the

event of our disolution as a Corps I am perfectly
convinc'd that, that Friendship so often employ'd
in my behalf is now exerting it's best endeavours in
accomplishing the primary Object, on which the
Fate of my ulterior efforts must greatly depend —
But should the Reg.^{t} be kept up till the King's pleasure relative to our being taken into His more
immediate Pay can be known, do you think it
impracticable for me to obtain the hon.^{r} of bearing
the Despatches on that Subject to the Ministry? or
if the first proposal is to be made at Head Quarters
to go there, near which I think I have a Friend
whose great Interest and powerful Connections
would render his good offices very prevailing. This
expedient has occurr'd to me by a proposal made to
me by severals of the Reg.^{t} for Detailing an Officer
to London to prosecute with that assiduity which the
pleasing view of Promotion would leave no room to
doubt, the most spirited perseverance in represent-
ing our Sufferings and Services — Should the War
continue the Difficulties in raising new Reg.^{ts} and
Recruit.^{s} those whose Effectives have been so much
diminish'd by severe Service will be so great and
the advantages resulting from taking a Regiment,
rais'd tolerably Disciplin'd and already in America,
must appear so strikingly obvious, that the Ministry
would on a proper Representation probably go into
it, as a Measure highly conducive to the Interest of
the Service, and at the same Time give an opportunity of obliging perhaps some of the Great Families in Britain by making Field Officers of some of
their Sons, Brothers or near Relations who may now

be Cap^{ts} in the Army, for 'tis certain that no Provincial Officers will at once be exalted to the Rank of Field Officers in the Service —

If Sir Jeffrey should of himself take us into the Pay of the Crown I would immediately rejoin the Reg^t — At any rate it seems to be pretty certain that the Colony will not retain us much longer in their Pay But supposing that we are kept up for the Winter I appeal to you or any other Military Judge whether the absence of Lt Col^o in Winter Quar^{trs} can be of any prejudice to the Service. If it cannot, if our standing even for that Time is doubtfull, if my going to London properly recommended may be of Service to the Corps in case the war continues and at all Events be of Service to myself, all which is very probable, I would fain hope the Governor may be prevail'd upon to hon^r me with his Letters to the Secretary of State; I can assure you that my being absent on this Service would be so infinitly remote from giving any umbrage to the Officers that many of them earnestly desire it — As my going to the Metropolis this Winter (where I think I could thro' the means of the Earles Bute and Loudon and some others of distinction in the army and about Court form a tolerable Interest) is of the utmost Importance to me, I doubt not but you'll be readily induc'd to forgive my anxious sollicitude about this most Interesting and decisive affair on the Success of which, in all human probability will greatly depend my future welfare or Misery, and will certainly be my derniere resource for making a vigorous push in the Military, on which, my heart is so much set —

In the happy Event of your Succeeding I would be extremely glad to receive the Letters open or under flying Seals that the General may be the more easily prevail'd on — and that no Time may be lost McNeil or Weedon will immediately send a Servant or an Express with them ——

May Heaven Bless you my dear Colonel and amply reward you for your steady and vivid Regard for

Your Truely Gratefull & mo: Affect^e

ROBERT STEWART

Allow me to remind you of the Bearer's ⎫
Affair, as you know him to be ancient & ⎬
Faithfull Servant to the Colony ⎭

P. S. If you can possibly procure the Govern^{rs} Letters I would be glad to receive some kind of Certificate from you specifying the Time I have been under your Command and my Behaviour during that Time   Be so good as to make my Complem^{ts} to Col^o Byrd for a Letter of the same kind while he Commanded the Reg^t which I cannot imagine he will deem any great Favour, and am persuaded that Genl Gage will not hesitate to write nor will Genl Monckton I'm pretty certain as well as severals of Rank in America — in fine I am resolv'd to spare no pains nor leave nothing unessay'd that yield even the most distant chance of promoting the Success of my Plann —

FROM CAPTAIN ROBERT STEWART.

LEWIS'S PLANTATION Decem.^r 14.th 1762

MY DEAR COLL.^o

I a few days ago had the pleasure to receive your obliging favour from Hoe's Ferry and am under the greatest concern for the return of your Lady's Indisposition, I would fain hope that the skill of the Faculty, your return and the excellent Weather will effect her recovery and perfectly reestablish her Health an acco.^t of which would afford me immense Joy — After rec.^t of yours I lost no Time in endeavouring to procure some of the Disbanded Soldiers to undertake your work in the manner you mention but so intoxicated were they with their temporary Liberty and the enjoyment of a few Shillings they had just rec.^d & which they were squandering in riot and Drunkenness that they were quite deaff to all proposals of that nature — Mr Lewis whose Plantation is within ¹/₂ Mile of the Ground on which we were encamp't could not for double Price prevail upon any of them to get a few Rails of which he was in great want, they swore they would not strike a stroke for any man till they should partake of the Christmass Frolicks, and then perhaps some of them would call upon you, however I with some difficulty prevail'd upon the Bearer Allen (who has been at Redstone Creek ever since Campaign 58) to wait upon you, in order to view the Ground in your Garden and propose the Terms upon wch he will Serve you in Quality of Gard.^r But with this Preliminary article of not Settling till after the approaching Holydays —

I yesterday Evening by M.r Posey rec.d your extreme kind favour from Williamsburgh and am really at loss for words to convey adequate Ideas of that pure Regard & genuine Gratitude your firm and uninterrupted Goodness has indelibly impress'd in my heart which is replete and will over flow with the warmest sentiments of the most exalted Esteem for you my best of Friends & dearest of acquaintances, Your own Letter is drest in that Stile and exhibits that ease candour and energy that clearly evinces it's proceeding immediately from the heart and is perfectly adapted to answer the Intention in the most efficacious manner — there are two Expressions in the Govern.s which I apprehend must take of the force and in a great measure destroy the end of a Recommendation, But as you Justly observe the Peace which will probably be concluded before I can make use of it will render every effort of this Nature ineffectual.

You no doubt have heard that the Assembly has given each Field Officer £100 — each Capt.t 75 & each Sub : £50 for the Expence they were at in Field Equipage & given all Six Months Pay — that they are to address The Throne in our Behalf & to grant a Sum to defray the Expence of the Officers that may be appointed to present the Address. Public rewards of Military Services conferr'd in so in genteel a manner must in future Wars be productive of the most happy consequences — I am told that B—t[1] according to his wonted modesty deems himself a proper person to present the address — for my part tho' I

---

1 Bullett ?

had previously determin'd on going home, yet a conscious inability of conducting ^myself with that propriety
and address the representative of a Corps should
display deterr'd me from dropping the most distant
hint even to my greatest Intimates in the Regim! —
So many favourable Circumstances must concur to
attract the notice of the Great so many difficulties to
be encounter'd which I fear a Peace will make quite
insuperable and leave no glimmering Ray of hope
for getting any thing done for the whole — Major
M:Neill is daily expected with the Cash whenever
he arrives I will set out for Head Quarters & will
soon be able to determine whether I shall continue
a Soldier or recommence Mohair,[1] in the Event of a
Peace, I think the latter will be the most eligible
as then in the Military way even hope the unfortunate's last comfort will be cut off — I believe I
need not say with how much reluctance I must leave
the Country without enjoying even a single hour's
Coversation with him I of all others esteem the most
to prevent this misfortune I as long as I possibly
could carefully avoided going to Fredericksb§ at
length the Col? S§ illness at disbanding of the Reg!
indispensably requir'd my going over 2 or 3 Times
therefore would not run the most distant risque of a
mere possibility of conveying the Infection to any of
that Family whose happiness will ever be dear to
me — God knows my dear Col? if ever we shall meet
again but this I am absolutely certain off that the
longest absence will not diminish that pure Affection & superlative Regard I have for you & I am too

---

1 A mercantile life.

well acquainted with the warmth of your Heart & the sincerity of your Friendship to imagine that the one can ever cool or the other abate. May Heaven Bless you & Mrs Washington with Health & every thing else you desire or may be necessary in completing y^r Felicity an acco^t of wch especially from yourself will always [be] an essential part of his who will ever remain with Supreme Esteem My Dear Sir Your Truely Affect^e Gratefull & mo: Obliged Servt

ROBERT STEWART

this Paper is so greasy that I fear you will hardly make out what is wrote on it

---

FROM CAPTAIN ROBERT STEWART.

MY DEAR COL^O

Two Days ago I arrived here, after a tedious Journey render'd doubly disagreeable by the excessive badness of the Roads & the extreme rigour of the weather, I was detain'd three Days at the River Susquhana, which was fill'd with such quantitys of driving Ice, as to make it impracticable for Boats, it at length shut up, and I at some risque cross'd upon the Ice. —

On my arrival at this place, I immediately waited upon Genl Monckton, who I found the same warm Friend I left him, he prevented my application, by enquiring what my Plan was, regretted my being so long unprovided for, and in the genteelest manner offer'd his best offices in promoting the Success of

whatever I might deem the most eligible, I therefore without reserve communicated my Intentions to him, which he approv'd off, and instantly applied in person to Sir Jeffery for his leave, for my going to London, where I shall carry G. M.^{s} warmest Recommendations: my Plan is, to propose to the Ministry (amongst whom I hope to find 2 good friends in Lord Bute and Mr Charles Townsend) to raise in America at my own Expence a Battalion of 5 Comp.^{ys} on condition of being made Major Commandant & having the appointment of the Officers which of late have been the common Terms, and however aspiring this may appear, yet I am assur'd by the most knowing here that the great demand for Men (for all thoughts of a Peace seems now to have vanish'd) the insuperable difficulties of getting them at home, the powerful Recommendations I shall carry with me, my Rank in the best of Provincial Corps, long Services &c.^{a} so well attested and strongly enforc'd, will more than probably secure the Success of my Plan — You'll by this Time pronounce me too sanguine, But allow me my dear Sir to assure you that Series of Disappointments sometimes when my hopes were rais'd to the highest pinnacle by the most flattering Prospect of Success have convinc'd me beyond any possibility of doubt how incompatible with reason & repugnant to common Prudence it would be to place my happiness on any unattain'd terrestial Blessing however alluring & near it may appear, yet as this yields a good probability I am willing to essay one vigourous Effort, and if I should not arrive at the summit of my views I may perhaps reach a Comp.^{y}

at the worst I can get a Purchass there with more
facility than here; I am therefore getting in readiness to embark with the next Packet which will ('tis
imagin'd Sail in about ten days) — I hope I need
not tell you how happy you will make me by charg-
ing me with the execution of any thing you may
have to do in London: I have tolerable knowledge
of most things you can want from thence, and I am
certain that none can take greater care in executing
them well, as the immense pleasure of obeying the
Commands of the Person I so highly revere, will
infinit'ly more than compensate for any pains it's
possible to be taken Your Letters will find me by
the underneath Direction — I beg my warmest Com-
plem.ᵗˢ & most hble Respects to Your Lady and
Family, Could my most ardent Wishes or anything
else within the utmost limit of my ability avail,
nothing should be wanting to completion of your
Joint Felicity, which will always promote mine God
Bless You My dear Colonel & believe me ever to be
with the most exalted Regard

Your Most Affectᵉ

&

Most Obliged hble Servᵗ

NEW YORK Janʸ 18ᵗʰ 1763 }   ROBERT STEWART

Please Direct for me To the Care ⎫
of Messʳˢ Levern & Stuart at   ⎪
the Corner of Eagle Street In great ⎬
Jermyne Street London   ⎭

Nothing new or entertaining here, I will do my-

self the great pleasure to write you again before I embark —

FROM CAPTAIN ROBERT STEWART

NEW YORK March 2ᵈ 1763 —

MY DEAR COL?

On the 18ᵗʰ of Jan⁷ I did myself the pleasure to write you a long Letter from hence, which by Post I sent under Cover to Mʳ Ramsay at Alexandria, and which I hope has long since got to hand, In that I inform'd you of the Plann I had form'd for my Promotion, the encouragement I met with, and the high probability there was of Success ; for sometime thereafter my affairs under the auspices of Genˡ Monckton wore a very promising aspect, and the different Steps previously necessary and leading to the commencement of my Operations were by his good Offices so far effected that I would have been ready to have embark'd with the first Packet when the dire accoᵗˢ of the Cessation Thunder'd on my disconcerted Mind and at once annihilated my Plann and Blasted my well grounded hopes, an event the more alarming to me, as ₍at₎ that Juncture it was so unexpected that the most sagacious here made no doubt of our Serving at least another Campaign,[1] which would have done for me, But as despondency can be of no Service and is often the mark of a weak mind, I would be willing like the drowning man to exert the remains of my enfeebled Strength in strug-

---

1 The definitive treaty of peace was concluded at Paris, February 10, 1763.

ling against the stream of adversity and as I foresaw the impossibility of getting anything done for me here I persever'd in the resolution I had taken of going home where I am told I shall have a much better chance to Purchass a Comp^y or if that should fail a Civil Employment, But my leave of absence has for various assign'd reasons been put off from Time to Time tho' that Genl M^n applied in person no less than three different Times — By my long detention here (where I am Subjected to an inevitable Expence I can very ill bear) I have not only lost perhaps the best opp^y for applying at home, but lost an opp^y of embarking on a Commercial Scheme, which my Mercantile Friends had a considerable Time ago concerted, and which I was either to have enter'd on or declin'd by the 1st of last Feb^{ry} You may perhaps think I ought to have Sold out or Resign'd — the 1st impossible as none will Buy in the Americans till their Fate is knowen and as to the 2^d when you consider that what I expect for my Lieu^{ty} must constitute a very considerable part of the Pittance I have to depend on, I'm persuaded you will think that a measure repugnant to prudence, so that I am oblig'd to make a Virtue of a necessity & wait with Patience — I am assur'd that the next Packet (which is daily expected) will bring Orders for the arrangement of the Troops &C^a & that I then will most certainly go home, where I will too probably stand in great need of that aid which you have often been Pleas'd to offer with that Polite candour and sincere warmth peculiar to genuine Friendship, which I with the less difficulty prevail upon myself to use

as all Danger of Death (except in the common way)
is now over & consequently yields me a much fairer
Prospect of reimbursing you than I had in the war.
But as I am not certain that I shall have reason for
it the Favour I would now Beg is that you will be
so good as to give me a Letter of Credit upon your
Correspondent in London for Four Hundred Pounds
Sterling in case I should want it,[1] You may probably
be surpris'd at my now applying for more than I did
3 years ago, to remove which, I will only inform
you that Capt Wood one of Genl M.^{ns} aid de Camps
who arriv'd from London a few Days ago says that
the price of Comp.^{ys} rose £500 — before he came
away and this you may absolutely rely on, that I
will take up as little as I can upon your Letter &
that no Expedient consistent with hon.^{r} will' [be] left
unessay'd to Pay you as soon as possible, But as all
human affairs are precarious I would likewise beg
that the Sum I may Draw upon you for may be so
enter'd in your Books that in the Event of your
Death (which I pray Heaven may long prevent)
your Heirs would not have it in their Power to distress me, One Copy of the Letter of Credit to be
sent by first Ship from Virginia under Cover to me

---

1 " I wish my dear Stewart that the circumstances of My Affairs woud have per-
mitted me to have given you an order upon any Person — in the world I might add —
for £400 with as much ease & propriety as you seem to require it, or even for twice
that sum if it woud make you easy ; . . . I do not urge these things [his own indebted-
ness] my dear Sir in order to lay open the distresses of my own Affairs, on the contrary
they shoud forever have remained profoundly secret to your knowledge did it not appear
necessary at this time to acquit myself in y.^{r} esteem, & to evince my inability of exceeding £300 a sum I am now labouring to procure by getting money to purchase Bills
of that am.^{t} to remit to yourself, that Mr Cary may have no knowledge of the transaction
since he expected this himself, and for which my regard for you will disappoint him —
A Regard of that high nature that I coud never see you uneasy without feeling a part
and wishing to remove the cause." — Washington to Stewart, April 27, 1763.

Directed agreeable to my last or to the Care of
Messrs Richard Oswald & Comp.^y Merch.^{ts} in London,
another Copy under Cover to me here and to be for-
warded by Mr Beverly Robinson by first Packet — I
will not attempt to Trouble you with appologizing for
this freedom as I so perfectly know your Sentiments
for which I hope Heaven will reward you & enable
me to prove worthy of it —

I am persuaded it will give you pleasure to know
that your old Acqua.^{ce} Governor Morris is appointed
Govr of N.^oCarolina — It is conjectur'd here that the
Commander in Chief will visit Virginia this Spring
Not a word of News here — I hope to have the
extreme pleasure of hearing from you before I'm long
in London I beg my most obliging & Respectfull
Complem.^{ts} to your Lady & Family & ever am with
Superlative Regard

My Dear Sir
Your Most Affect.^e & mo : Obliged hble Servt
ROBERT STEWART

FROM CAPTAIN ROBERT STEWART.

NEW YORK June 6.th 1763

MY DEAR COL.^O

Both your favours of the 27th April & 2^d May, Cov-
ering your Bills for £302 – – Ster.^g I rec^d from M.^r
Robinson last week and would have instantly acknow-
ledg'd the rec.^t of them but that I knew the Bearer
would set out for Virginia in a few days which is a
better and perhaps a safer conveyance than by Post

the irregularity of which I have long since been convinc'd off — But where shall I find words to convey
an adequate Idea of those emotions which your most
Affectionate Letters has caus'd in a heart replete
with the most lively Sentiments of genuine Gratitude
or how can I sufficiently admire that exalted Friendship which absence the bane of common Friendships
encrease, which is invigorated by difficulties, and
shines with additional lustre when put to the severest
trial? — the most pleasing reflections certainly result
from viewing that uncommon Species of happiness I
enjoy in having such a Friend, yet it gives me the
deepest concern that my unhappy Situation in Life
forc'd me to do what has Subjected you to many
inconveniencies to lessen them in some degree I will
leave no expedient unessay'd and will not use the
Bills for myself till every thing else has fail'd

Since my last I have not been able to get any
thing done I have been put off from the arrival of
one Packet to another at length was told that I must
remain here till the distribution and arrangement of
the Troops arrives for which there is yet no Order
tho' a man of war with them has been for some time
expected — had Sir Jeff. told General Monckton when
he first applied for me that I could not go home I
would have sold out which I could then have done
without much difficulty and in all probability would
'ere now have either been provided for in the Service
or Settled in Business But by giving me hopes from
Time to Time he has not only involv'd me in that
perplexity inseperable from uncertainty but Subjected
me to a very heavy Expence a great part of which I

to my affairs, but Sir Jeff always found new reasons
for my detention, I could not by any means obtain
his Liberty, nor did he give me an absolute denial,
but kept me in the most painfull suspence, and disagreeable attendance, from the middle of last Jan.ʸ till
the latter end of last Month, at length when I little
expected it he gave me his leave in writing accom-
panied by a heap of Friendly professions (which I
set down for nothing) and as the place where I had
suffer'd so much uneasiness had long since become
perfectly disagreeable to me I embrac'd the earliest
opp.ʸ of getting away, and arriv'd here yesterday to
take my Passage in a Ship which I was told would
sail in a few days for London but I find that none
will sail from hence in less than three weeks, for
that place where I still continue determ'd to make
a vigourous effort for a Comp.ʸ I readily foresee the
most insuperable difficulties with which the Peace
has obstructed the road to Military preferment But
as I think I can rely upon Gen.¹ Monckton's Interest
and some others of distinction and as the necessary
Regulations for the due Government of the Con-
quered Countries will occasion a number of new
Appointments both Civil and Military I would fain
hope I shall be able to procure something genteel at
any rate it is my last resource — should I fail the
attempt will indeed be ₍against₎ me but in my situation I
think it would be timidity rather than prudence not
to make a Trial ——
    The Engineers Gordon and Basset are ₍here₎ and pre-
sent their Complem.ᵗˢ to you they have both obtain'd

leave to go home; Basset acted as aid de Camp in that very fortunate Affair near Bussie Run [1] and extols the firm coolness uns[h]aken intrepidity and vast alacrity of the Highlanders which compos'd that little Army even to a hyperbole — certain it is that nothing could be more fortunate for these Colonies than the hardly to be hop'd for Success of that day, as the very existence of the back Country depended on the safety of that Convoy for ('tis said) that Fort Pitt and consequently all it's dependencies must have fallen for want of Provisions and Ammunition the consequences of which especially to the midle Colonies would have been dreadfull beyond description, there may be reasons for neglecting a Post of such vast importance which was the cause of the last war and which has cost Great Britain and Her Colonies so much Bloud and Treasure to acquire and maintain and on whose safety the Lives and Properties of so many Thousands of His Majesty's Subjects depended, But Success gives the most alureing gloss even to the most egregious Blunders [2] —

---

1 Immediately after peace was concluded with France in 1763, there was a general uprising of the western tribes of Indians, who, after capturing nearly all the frontier forts, united in a fierce attack upon Fort Pitt. Captain Ecuyer, in command there, held the fort under an exhausting blockade for over a month. Colonel Bouquet, who was sent to his relief, was attacked by, but overcame, the savages at Bushy Run, within twenty miles of Fort Pitt, near the headwaters of Turtle Creek.

2 " Things being in that situation I received orders to march with the above troops, the only force the General could collect at that time for the relief of this fort [Fort Pitt], which was in great want of provisions, the little flour they had being damaged.

" In that pressing danger the provinces refused to give us the least assistance. Having formed a convoy, I marched from Carlisle the 18th of July with about 460 rank and file, being the remains of the 42d and 77th regiments, many of them convalescents. I left thirty men at Bedford, and as many at Ligonier, where I arrived on the 2d instant. Having no intelligence of the enemy, I determined to leave the waggons at

FROM CAPTAIN ROBERT STEWART.

My Dear Sir

In my last which has distanced this much farther than I intended I gave you a circumstantial Detail of Lord Egmont's Plan,[1] the motives that induc'd us to Join him, and the various Causes that occasion'd it's overthrow; upon which, we resumed our original Claim at the Board of Trade, where it was intimated to us by the First Lord Commissioner that, had we stood upon our own Legs, we might probably 'ere then have been in possession of our Grants; But as the value and fertility of that Island, had made much noise in the Nation, and occasioned some heartburn-ings amongst the Great, it was indispensably neces-sary for the Board to proceed with Caution, and therefore, had determined to Recommend it to His Majesty that no Grants should be made till the ex-tent and Contents of the Island could be exactly ascertained; for which purpose, they had sent out Cap.[t] Holland (Surveyor general for America) with four Assistants to make an exact Survey of it, after which (by their Orders) the whole is to be laid off

---

[1] While men were taken up with the politics of the age, there was a Minister so smitten with the exploded usages of barbarous times, that he thought of nothing less than reviving the feudal system. This was the Earl of Egmont (John Perceval, second Earl of Egmont), who had actually drawn up a plan for establishing that absurd kind of government in the island of St. John. He printed several copies of his scheme, and sent them about to his brother peers. And so little were they masters of the subject, and so great was the inattention of the Ministry to the outlying parts of our empire, that his Lordship, in the following year, had prevailed with the Council to suffer him to make the experiment, if General Conway had not chanced to arrive at Council and expose the folly of such an undertaking, which occasioned its being laid aside. Lord Egmont was such a passionate admirer of those noble tenures and customs, that he rebuilt his house at Enmere in Sommersetshire in the guise of a castle, moated it round, and prepared it to defend itself with cross-bows and arrows, against the time in which the fabric and use of gunpowder shall be forgotten. — Walpole's *Memoirs*.

into Lots of twenty thousand Acres, as near in value with respect to soil and situation as it will admit of, and if practicable each to contain some part of the improved Lands and Sea Coast, as the Island is long and narrow, no part of it being 15 Miles from Navigation, and the French Inhabitants having settled in a very Detach'd manner these Instructions can with the more facility be in a great measure be obeyed, however to avoid every inconvenience of that kind as much as possible, Each Adventurer is to have a small Lot for Warehouses &c. either on Port-Joy or St Pierre the principal Harbours, where Towns are to be built, the Lots to be mark'd and Number'd upon the Map, Capt Holland is to make of the Island, and to be drawn for by the Adventurers or, their Agents, at the Board of Trade; the last acco^{ts} the Board rec^d from Capt Holland he was in hopes to finish his Survey by the First of next Month so that by the last of October we may expect that this very tedious affair which has cost, so much Time, trouble, attendance and expence will be finally adjusted I flatter myself to our advantage and satisfaction —

I fear you will think it strange that I should so readily have engaged in a Land Scheme, and under a number of Difficulties so long persever'd in what must appear to you not only incompatible with my views in the Army to which I was almost an enthusiast, but, repugnant to my former Sentiments of Life, But some of my Friends here so clearly shewed the great and almost immediate advantages that must result from Settling in a Fertile Island water'd with fine Rivers which abound with Salmond and other excellent Fish, indented with commodious Har-

calculated for publick utility than your private Emolument; I dread that the Expence incurr'd by this undertaking may occasion your missing that Sum you so generously furnished me with, which would give me excessive uneasiness: Drawing it from me before I am settled, would distress me extremely, But this you may absolutely rely on, that neither you nor your Heirs can run any risque of loosing a farthing of either principal or Interest, and that the moment I am able (of which you shall have the earliest Intelligence) I will with infinite thankfulness reimburse you —

As for News I beg leave to refer you to the Bearer Col? Mercer who returns to Collect a Tax upon his native Land, the Mode of imposing which, we are told, the people of America in general, and the Virginians in particular, look on as an infringement of their Priviledges, which has occasioned such a ferment, that a Majority of their Representives in a Legislative Capacity, made some very warm and bold Resolves, Printed Copies of which are handed about in this place but it is asserted that the last and most violent of them is spurious —

	Contra . . . C^r.		
1763.			
May	By Sundry Sums of £3. put in by Messrs Lewis Basset, Walker & myself in our first trip to the Dismal Swamp	12	——
Nov^r.	By my quota of £600. voted for carrying on the Work of Draining &c^a	50	——
1764.			
May	By Cash of Col? Field^s Lewis	20	——
	By the Contra. 100 Bar^{ls} of Corn — not wanted . . .	62 .. 10	—
		£144 .. 10	—

Here the whole Political frame has for some time been strangely agitated, by the most unexpected Revolutions; the principals of the new Administration have been for some time appointed, and their Friends are by degrees taking possession of the inferior offices, occupied by those of the late Ministry; with respect to the Abilities, Parliamentary Interest and permanency of the present, people are so much and generally divided in their opinions that time can alone discover the rectitude or fallacy of their different Sentiments which are maintained with such heat on both sides; How happy My dear Colonel are they who indepe[n]dent of all Parties

	To Value of my Slaves (provided for Drain⁵ the Dismal Swamp) above yᵉ average Price of them	52 .. 18 .. 4
Decʳ 16.	To Cash paid Colᵒ Lewis for my quota of £480 voted by the Company . Decʳ 16ᵗʰ 1764	40 ———
		£92 .. 18 .. 4

1765.

Octʳ	To Cash allowed in Accᵗ with Colᵒ Lewis for yᵉ Contra Shing⁵	35 ———
1766	To Ditto paid Mʳ Jnᵒ Washington by Colᵒ Lewis . .	25 ———
May 3.	To Ditto pᵈ — Ditto . . myself	25 ———
Decʳ.	To Cash paid Miles Riddick's Exʳˢ being the first payment due for Land boᵗ of them	100 .
1767 Apˡ.	To Cash pᵈ Colᵒ Field⁵ Lewis — my proportion towards the first paymᵗˢ for yᵉ above Land	17 .. 7 .. 10
	To Ditto pᵈ Dᵒ.. being a Balᵉ recᵈ from the Contra Gentlemen	4 .. 7 .. 0
		£206 .. 14 .. 10

	To my Expˢ going & returnˢ to the Swamp in Novʳ 1766	1 .. 2 .. 10
	To Dᵒ. Dᵒ. going &cᵃ in Apˡ 1767	1 .. 12 .. 6
Octʳ 1767	To half of Colᵒ Lewis's and my Expˢ to yᵉ Swamp this Trip .. the whole being £1 .. 15 .. 9	.. 17 .. 10
	To my propⁿ of the last paymᵗ for Riddick's Land . .	17 .. 11 .. 4
	To my Expˢ to the Dismal Swamp in Octʳ 1768 . . .	2 .. 16 .. 8
1768.		
	To Cash pᵈ Colᵒ. Lewis for my part of yᵉ late Speakers share in yᵉ dismˡ Swamp	56 .. 2 .. 2
		80 .. 3 .. 4

can, collected within themselves, enjoy that tranquility and Peace of mind which these others must ever be Strangers to? I pray Heaven may ever Bless you and yours with that and every other Species of Felicity; I beg you will be pleased to render my Dutifull and affectionate Respects to Your Lady — I often think with immense satisfaction on the many very pleasant days I have so agreeably passed in your most desirable Company, and severely regrett my hard Fate in being deprived of so inestimable a Blessing, Tho' it is so far from proving impossible that I am big with the pleasing hope that when I get affairs properly arrang'd at St John's to

	By Cash of Jn.º Robinson Esq.ʳ whose Slaves were under the average price	52 .. 18 .. 4
1764		
Dec.ʳ 16	By my quota of £480 voted this day for carrying on our operation's in the D. Swamp	40 ————
		92 .. 18 .. 4
1765.		
June 12.	By 70,300. Shingles of M.ʳ Jn.º Washington @ 10/ . .	35 ——— 0
1766.	By my proportion of £300 Voted	25 ———
May 3.	By D.º .. D.º of £300 Voted this day	25 ———
Dec.ʳ	By Cash — viz. £17 .. 7 .. 10 rec.ᵈ myself, from each of the following Gentlemen — to wit W.ᵐ & Thom.ˢ Nelson Esq.ʳˢ & M.ʳ Waters (for self & Mead) . £52 .. 3 .. 6	
Dec.ʳ	By D.º from Doct.ʳ Waker .. Col.º Tucker & M.ʳ Farley, each £17 .. 7 .. 10. by the hands of Col.º Fielding Lewis . . .	52 .. 3 .. 6
		104 .. 7 .. 0
	By my own prop.ⁿ of the paym.ᵗ	17 .. 7 .. 10
		£206 .. 14 .. 10
	By my Interest on the Land purchased of M.ʳ Miles Riddicks Estate	17 .. 11 .. 4
	By my Ditto in the late Speakers Share of the Swamp .	56 .. 2 .. 2
1772		
Jan. 1	By Bal.ᵗ carr.ᵈ to Acc.ᵗ in Ledger B	6 .. 9 .. 10
		£80 .. 3 .. 4

(Washington's Ledger.)

have the immense pleasure of making an excursion from thence to Mount Vernon — I flatter myself that I shall towards the beginning of next Summer embark for S! Johns properly equip'd for effecting a small Settlement there, long 'ere then I hope to have the great pleasure of hearing from you, when you are pleased to write be so good as to Direct to the Care of Mess.ᵣˢ Savern & Stuart Great Jermyn Street S! James London —

I am ever with the most exalted Esteem & entire Regard

My Dear Col?
Your truely & unalterably Affect.ᵉ &
Most Gratefully Obliged hble Serv.ᵗ

ROBERT STEWART

LONDON August 18ᵗʰ }
1765 }

I beg my most obliging Complem.ᵗˢ to your Brothers, Col. Fairfax M.ʳ Kirkpatrick and the rest of my good Acquaint.ˢ with you —

<hr>

FROM MR. JOSEPH DAVENPORT.

BULSKIN Oct! 16ᵗʰ 1765 —

S.ᴿ

I this day fill'd the pond at home with hemp and Tomorrow intend to fill One that I have at the Lower Quarter tho I am doubtful it will not hold all the hemp besides, what Bore Seed and that I know not what to do with for by than this comes out the water will be too Cold — the Seed turns out Very indifferently

I have Cleaned about 25 Bushels and do not believe
I shall have above 7 or 8 more I have Broke very
Little hemp Since I wrote by Giles But Expect to be
at it next week with Chief of the hands as Connell
has made it so late I have sent all the Buter and
Cheese which is 346ᵗᵇ of Nett Butter the Caske being
12ᵗᵇ Fare Each and 81ˡᵇ Cheese. & should be glad
to know what Mʳˢ MᶜCarmick is to be allowed for
her part and whether I may settle with her. as she
seems to be in want of her pay I in hopes you may
have heard by this time whether may depend on
going under Mʳ Valentine or not and if not if it is
not too Late I would Serve Colᵒ Fairfax in this
County, and as ᴧagreed to Leave it to you to Settle
the day if you will be kind Enough to take the
Trouble on yʳ self I will enter into any Article you
and he shall agree on. and Esteem it a particular
favour.

> from Sʳ your very Hble Servᵗ
>
> Joˢ Davenport

N. B. the Negroes are all
well at present tho Several of
them have had a touch of ague
I myself have had 3 or 4 fits
of it But am in hopes it has left me

FROM COLONEL GEORGE MASON.[1]

GUNSTON-HALL 23ᵈ Decemʳ 1765.

GENTLEMEN

Inclosed is the Scheme I promised you for altering the method of replevying Goods under Distress for Rent: I thought it necessary to explain fully the Land-lord's Right by the common Law, to shew that our Act of Assembly[2] was a mere Matter of Indulgence, & that an Alteration of it now will be no Incroachment upon the Tenant: the first part of it has very little to do with the Alteration proposed, & only inculcates a Doctrine I was always fond of promoting, & which I cou'd wish to see more generally adopted than it is like to be: the whole is indeed much longer than it might have been, but that you will excuse as a natural Effect of the very idle Life I am forced to lead. I beg you will alter such parts of it as either of you think exceptionable.

If I had the Act of Assembly obliging our Vestry to pay for the Glebe[3] &c. I wou'd prepare a petition for Redress, & get it signed in Time.

Wishing the Families at Belvoir & Mount Vernon all the Mirth & Happiness of the approaching Festival, I am Gentᵐ

Yʳ most obdᵗ Hble Serᵗ

G MASON

---

[1] Addressed, " To Colᵒ Geo: Fairfax & Colᵒ Geo: Washington."
[2] Hening, vol. vi. p. 9.   [3] Hening, vol. vi. p. 89.

Scheme for Replevying Goods and Distress for Rent.[1]

The policy of encouraging the Importation of free people & discouraging that of Slaves has never been duly considered in this Colony, or We shou'd not at this Day see one Half of our best Lands in most parts of the Country remain unsettled, & the other cultivated with Slaves ; not to mention the ill Effect such a practice has upon the Morals and Manners of our people : one of the first Signs of the Decay, & perhaps the primary Cause of the Destruction of the most flourishing Government that ever existed was the Introduction of great Numbers of Slaves — an Evil very pathetically described by the Roman Historians — but 'tis not the present Intention to expose our Weakness by examining this Subject too freely.

That the Custom of leasing Lands is more beneficial to the Community than that of settling them with Slaves is a maxim that will hardly be denied in any free Country ; tho' it may not be attended with so much imediate profit to the Land-holder : in proportion as it is more useful to the public, the Invitations from the Legislature to pursue it shou'd be stronger : — no Means seem so natural as securing the payment of Rents in an easy & effectual Manner : the little Trouble & Risque attending this Species of Property may be considered as an Equivalent to the greater profit arising from the Labour of Slaves, or any other precarious & troublesom Estate. The common-Law (independant of any Statute) gives the Land-lord a right to distrain upon anything on his Land for the Rent due ; that is, it puts his Remedy into his own Hands : but as so unlimited a power was liable to be abused, it was found necessary to punish the Abuse by penal Statutes, made in terrorem, to preserve Justice, & prevent the Oppression which the poor might otherwise suffer from the rich, not to destroy the Land-lord's Right, which still remained unimpeached, and has not only been exercised in this Colony from its first Settlement, but has obtained in our Mother-Country from Time immemorial. Uninterrupted life

---

1 Inclosed in letter of December 23.

& long Experience carry with them a Conviction of general Utility.

The fluctuating State ₐof our Trade, the Uncertainty of our Markets & the Scarcity of Money frequently render it impracticable for the Debtor to Raise Money out of his Effects to discharge a sudden & perhaps unexpected Judgement, & have introduced a Law giving the Debtor a Right to replevy his Goods under Execution by Bond with Security (approved by the Creditor) to pay the Debt & Costs with Interest in three Months; which Bonds are returnable to the Clerk's Office whence the Execution issued, to remain in the Nature of Judgements, & final Executions may be obtain'd upon them when due by a Motion to the Court, with ten Days notice to the partys. The Legislature, considering Distresses for Rents in the same Light with Executions for common Debts, has thought fit to extend the same Indulgence to them; tho' it would not be hard to shew that the Cases are by no means similar, & that the Reasons which are just in the former do not hold good in the latter: by comparing the Laws there also appears such an Inconsistency in that relating to replevin Bonds for Rent as may render the Method prescribed difficult if not impracticable; there being no previous Record (as in the Case of Executions) the Bonds do not seem properly returnable to the Clerk's Office, nor is that Matter clearly express'd or provided for in the Act. This has not hitherto been productive of much Inconvenience; tho' contrary to the Course & Spirit of the common-Law, the Land-lord may thereby be brought into a Court of Judicature before he can get the Effect of a just & legal Distress; but in our present Circumstances it will occasion manifest Injustice.

If the Officer making a Distress, upon being offered Security, refuses to take a Bond for Want of Stamp'd Paper, the Goods of the Tenant must be imediately exposed to Sale, & he deprived of the Indulgence intended by the Act of Assembly.

If the Officer takes a replevin Bond as usual, the Land-lord will lose his Rent, the Tenant then having it in his power to keep him out of it as long as he pleases, for in the present Confusion & Cessation of Judicial proceedings the Land-lord will not have an Opportunity of applying to Court for an Execution when the

Friends all the Advantages of the ready money
Duties —

I have the honour to be with due Respect
Dr Sir
Your most Obed^t Servt
WILL HUNTER

FROM COLONEL BERNARD MOORE.[1]

[A Copy.]

MY DEAR SIR,

Your favour received & should have answered it
long before this, but expected to have had the pleasure of seeing you at Williamsburg this Court, but
am prevented by a long spell of the ague and fever,
and am so unwell as not to attend the Gen! Court.
I am extremely obliged to you for your kind offer in
taking my bond for principal & interest of my old
Bond. I declare to you it is not in my power to collect in what moneys are due to me or else should be
able to pay you the interest. I shall be obliged to
you to let me know what sum I owe you and then I
will give you the bond with security; such as I have
no doubt you will approve of. Your great kindness
to me heretofore convinces me that you will not distress a family so large as mine is, and you may
depend no one shall fall on more speedy and honest

---

[1] Bernard Moore, of " Chelsea," son of Augustine and Elizabeth Moore, married
Anne Catharine, daughter of Governor Spotswood. One of their daughters married
Charles Carter, of Shirley, and was grandmother to General Robert Edward Lee.
Bernard Moore was for many years a member of the Virginia House of Burgesses.
Brock, in the *Spotswood Papers*, connects Colonel Augustine Moore, " of Chelsea,"
Virginia, with Sir Thomas More, of "Chelsea," England.

methods to extricate themselves out of their troubles than I will do.[1]

With great truth

Y.^r Affec.^t

BER.^D MOORE

21 Oc.^t 1766

FROM COLONEL THOMAS MOORE.

KING WILLIAM Octr 21. 1766 —

DEAR SIR

Haveing from time to time beg d your Indulgence in regard to the money I owe you and haveing as often reced it with the greatest kindness and good nature I have not now the face to ask any longer time but least you should think I have bin faulty & have not truly indeavoured to procure it I must assure you I have done every thing in my power to collect the money for you and tho I have severall thousands due me for great part of which I have brought suits above two years ago but to my great mortifica- tion and disapointment I have not yet got Judge-

---

1 Coll.^o Bernard Moore . . . . D.^{rs}

1758	To your Bond given to (Mrs Custis) .. for	£1400 ———
May 12 ⎰ 3		
1761 ⎱	To/years Interest on Ditto a 5 p/.^t p.^r an	210 ———
		£1610

1763 ⎰	To your Bill of Excha : on Mr Thos Usher returned ⎰	Sterl.^g	
	under protest — dated 30.th Ap.^l 1763 . . . for . . . ⎱	£100 ———	
May 1 ⎱	To Int.^t from the date of ye above Bill untill now .	40 ———	
1767			
		140 .. 0 .. 0	
	To Cost of protest	− .. 4 .. 3	
		£140 .. 4 .. 3	

ments   Others I have not sued but intreeted and persuaided but to no purpose as money was so scarce it could not be got by them nay if they sold their Estates (as some offered to do) they could_∧^{not}expect above half price In short Sir I promis you I have not bin Idle and can prove if required what I have mentioned to be realy the truth ———

I am Assured now I shall have Judgements very soon and get my money and others that are not sued have promis'd considerable sums shall be paid I therefore have all the reason in_∧^{the}World to beleave the time draws near that I shall wate on you with the money & with my acknowledgements — As to the interest due you, my intention & full purpose is to pay Interest on that also as the severall sums become due — I flatter my self the want of the money ~~will~~ for a few months longer will be no material hurt to you If you should want it to purchase Negroes rather than you should be disapointed I will furnish you out of my own   I only mention this to show you I am ready and willing to do every thing in my

Contra . . . . Cʳˢ

By my Bond drawn payable to Collᵒ. Spotswoods Exʳ. .	£123	———
By your Order on Jnᵒ Robinson Esqʳ	87	———
By your Bond Assigned to Miss Custis	1400	

£1610

1767 May 1 { By Miss Custis allowed her in yᵗ Bond with Jnᵒ. Baylor Esqʳ. Security for £1338 .. 11 .. 0   My part of which being . . . . } £140 .. 4 .. 3

£140 .. 4 .. 3

(Washington's Ledger.)

power_∧keep you from sustaining any damage on my
Acco.^t.¹ — I am very respectfully
Dr Sir
Your ob.^t hble Ser.^t
THO.^S MOORE

NB.

If I should be disapointed
in part of the money I expect to
receve my Crops as_∧ I can_∧ them
sold I hope will be more than make
up the deficientecy

1758	1 Col.º Tho.ª Moore . . . D.ʳ		
May 2	To his Bond to Martha Custis for	£1400	——
	1 years Interest of Ditto	70	——
		1470	——
1760 May 2	To Ball.º p.ʳ Contra	1400	——
Nov. 4	To Interest of Ditto to this date	105 .. 13 .. 4	
1760		1505 .. 13 .. 4	
Nov.ʳ 4	To Ball.º p.ʳ Contra	1005 .. 13 .. 5	
1761 Nov.ʳ 7	To Interest on Ditto	50 .. 12 .. 11	
		1056 .. 7 .. 4	
Nov.ʳ 7	To Ball.º p.ʳ Contra	806 .. 7 .. 4	
1770 June 11	{ To Interest thereon to this date, viz 8 y.ʳˢ 7 Months & 4 days . . . . }	345 .. 17 .. 10	
		1152 .. 5 .. 2	
1770 June 11	To Ball.º p.ʳ Contra	1048 .. 5 .. 2	
	To Cash to Carter Braxton Esq.ʳ	1 .. 14 .. 10	
		1050 — —	
	To my Credit as above	10 .. 0 .. 0	
1772 Jan 1	To amount bro.ᵗ from Ledger A	204 .. 10 .. —	

FROM COLONEL BERNARD MOORE.

Dear Sir

My inclination to do the Strictest Justice to the Several Gentlemen to whom I am indebted & the distrest state of the Country making it impossible for some of them to wait untill the produce of my Estate can raise sufficient to satisfy the demands upon it, has induced me to make Sale of all my lands in King William to clear my incumbrances. I am willing to flatter my self from our long acquaintance that you have some regard for me and my large family, and

1759	Contra . . . Cᵣ —		
	By Cash	70 .. 0 .. 0	
	By Ballᵉˢ carrᵈ to new Accᵗ	1400 ————	
		1470 ————	
1760			
Novᵣ 4	By Cash of Jnᵒ Robinson Esqᵣ	500 ————	
	By Ballᵉ carrᵈ to new Accᵗ	1005 .. 13 .. 5	
		1505 .. 13 .. 5	
1761	By Jnᵒ Robinson Esqᵣ	250 ————	
Novᵣ 7			
	By Ballᵉ. carrᵈ to new Accᵗ . . . , ...	806 .. 7 .. 4	
		1056 .. 7.. 4	
1770	By Sundries boᵗ at his Sale — viz		
June 11	Negro Frank . . . . £31 .. 0 .. 0		
	Ditto boy James . . . . 55 ———		
	A Bay Mare . . . . 8 .. 5 —		
		94 .. 5 —	
	By a Credit to himself at the above Sale . . . . . 10 ———		
	By Ballᵉ. carrᵈ to new Accᵗ	1048 .. 0 .. 2	
		1152 .. 5 .. 2	
	By Carter Braxton Esqᵣᵣˢ Bond to Miss Martha P. Custis . . . . }	1050 ———	
	By amᵗ carrᵈ to Ledger B — folio 17	10 .. 0 .. 0	
	By Loss	10 .. 0 .. 0	

(Washington's Ledger.)

that if its in your power to serve me that I may hope for your kind assistance to promote the Sale, Should it suit yourself to lay out monys in the purchase of Land perhaps those I intend to sell may answer your purpose. The Lands I propose to sell is where I live, the Tract contains about 3500 Acres, its of a long square, from River to River about 3 miles long & about 2 miles in width, the quallity you partly know, and if you will be kind enough to come and see the whole your good Judgement will govern you in what manner to Act. there is 500 fine bearing Apple trees, about 2000 fine young Peach trees that will begin to bear next Summer. The plantations for 20 or 30 hands in as good order for Croping as any in the Country. Buildings on the plantations of all sorts and in good order, many of them new. The house I live in is as good as new, compleatly finished 5 rooms on a floor, garden, out Houses &c., all new, and in good order. If this tract should suit you, or you should think proper to purchase it for Master Custis I shall be glad to see you down here, I am most sure when you come to see the conveniences, and the Situation of the Land that we shant disagree[1]

My best complements attend on you & my old friend M.rs Washington and am

Dear Sir

Your Most Aff Serv.t

BER.D MOORE

29.th Dec.r 1766.

---

1 "Chelsea," the home of Colonel Bernard Moore, was situated on the Mattapony River, in the parish of St. John, King William County.

FROM DR. WILLIAM SAVAGE.[1]

DUMFRIES 25th May 1767 —

SIR

I was cal d away last Monday upon Business that I neither foresaw, nor coud postpone, tho' I had appointed both Col. Lee & M[r] Payne to be at Alexandria that day, the latter of whom kept himself in readiness till late in the Evening to accompany me — I am obliged to be at next Essex Court upon very urgent Business which also happens to be ~your~ Alexandria Court Week & perhaps the following Court I may be disappointed or it may happen not to be Conven[t] for the two Gentlemen that I have already proposed for the Counter Security of You, & Col. Fairfax to attend — As I am now really uneasy till I can make you think yourselves perfectly Indemnifyed I shall propose to you that these 2 gent together with one or more of some Note in this County shall Join in a Conditional Bond for the particular sum that you are already bound for which you may depend shall be properly drawn by some Att[y] & witnessed by two, or more People, I shall inform myself of the exact sum by examining the Record —. This will be very Convenient for me to have done next Monday being our Court Day & if you think it suffic[tly] Satisfactory it will be doing me a particular favor — otherwise I shall endeavour (however Inconven[t]

---

1 The emigrant ancestor of the Savage family in Virginia was probably Thomas Savage, who came over in the John and Frances in 1608. He married Hannah ——. Their only son John, who was born in 1624, was a magistrate of the Colony, and a member of the House of Burgesses.

to myself or others) to attend next Alexandria Court
& have the requisite decree.[1]

I am Sir y.^r

most obed.^t

hble Servt

W.^{M.} SAVAGE.

FROM MR. HUGH STEPHENSON.[2]

BULSKIN July 1.st. 1767

SIR /

I am sorry it was not in my power to Come Down
according to prommise my bisness Lay so ilconve-
nent that I Cold not Come which I hope your Hon-
nour will Excuse me for not Comeing at that time
and you may Depend upon my Comeing in two or
three weeks at the Longest the man that Lives on
the Cole Plantation be Low me is now down and is

---

[1] MOUNT VERNON 27th May 1767.

SIR

The Security, and manner of giving it, propos'd in yours of the 25th will be perfectly satisfactory to me, if any Inconvenience attends the other method of doing it;
but as Col^{o.} Fairfax is equally concernd, and from home, I woud choose to answer for
myself only; persuaded nevertheless, that it will be agreeable to him also to give you
as little trouble as possible on this head: In the meantime, and in his absence, let me
desire that this matter may not interfere with any other business you may have on
hand, or give cause for uneasiness: — it affords none to me, & I dare venture to say
the same for Col^{o.} Fairfax. —

I was in hopes before this to have received money from Mess. Carlyle & Adam,
& therewith dischargd my Bond to the late Rev^{d.} Mr. Green, — they have hitherto
disappointed me — but having Mr. Adam's promise to see you in a few days for this
purpose, I hope he will fulfill it in paying the money. —

I am Sir

Y.^r Most H^{ble} Servt

G WASHINGTON.

Washington's reply to Doctor Savage.

[2] Hugh Stephenson, son of Richard Stephenson, of Frederick County, was, on
Washington's recommendation, appointed in March, 1776, colonel of the regiment of
Virginia riflemen, but died shortly after his appointment.

to Let me now when he returns what time M.ʳ Fairfax will be at home that I mant miss of him when I go Down — mr Crawford desired me to Let you now that he had spoke to a woman to Spin for you but I do not think it is proper to send her before that he had an oppertunity to send som of her work to you that you mite see if she would sute you

I am Sir your Humble ˢᵗ

HUGH STEPHENSON

FROM CAPTAIN WILLIAM CRAWFORD.[1]

Sep.ʳ 29.ᵗʰ 67 by ——

Dᴿ SIR/

I was favoured, with two Letters from you, one dated y.ᵉ 13.ᵗʰ and y.ᵉ other the 17.ᵗʰ instant [2] ——

I believe I can procure you What Land you want in Pensilvania, but cannot tell what Quantity they will allow in a survey, I shall inform my self they first Oppertunity — I have bin through great part of the good Land on the North Side of the Monongahalia, as far up as the mouth of Cheet River, on both sids of Youchagania [3] to the mouth and all its

---

[1] Captain, afterwards Colonel, William Crawford was born in Virginia about 1722. He moved with his family to Fayette County, Pennsylvania, in 1766. Captain Crawford served under Washington all through the Forbes campaign of 1758; he also took an active part in "Dunmore's War" of 1774, and in 1776 entered the Revolutionary service as lieutenant-colonel of the Fifth Virginia Regiment. As a surveyor also he held many positions of importance. In 1782 he commanded the expedition to Sandusky against the Ohio Indians, by whom he was taken prisoner, and tortured to death. His aid-de-camp on this occasion, Major John Rose (Baron Rosenthal), in a journal of the expedition, describes Colonel Crawford as "a man of Sixty and upwards. . . . In his private Life, kind and *exceedingly* affectionate; in his military character, personally Brave, and patient of hardships. . . . As a Commanding Officer, cool in danger, but not systematical. . . . No military Genius & no man of Letters."

[2] Washington's second letter was dated the 21st.   [3] Youghiogany.

Branches on the western Side of the Mountains Chief part of the good Land is taken up between the two rivers when I cam down there was som un setle.^d yeat very good which I think would Please you, Few or none had settled over the Monongahalia, as they did not care to setle there for fear of Disturbing the Endians [1] — I have pitch^d upon a fine peace of Land on a Camp called Shirtees [2] Creek near the head about 25 Miles from Fort pitt, it Emtys into the Ohio about 5 miles below the fort on the south side, the Land Consist of Choice Bottems from a Quarter to half a mile wide, the up Land is as Lavel, as Comon for that Country to be Rich and well timber^d a good streem, fit for water works, there may be had one Tract about 2 or 3 thousand Acres or better, I beleve, where I was on the Creek, and I am told by the Endians it holds good Down to the mouth of the Creek, you may if ^you Please Joyne me in that, if no Person has taken it before I get out, the Chiefest Danger is from the Fort [3] as I understand there has been some surveyors gone up Latly from Pensilvania in order to Run out some Land, but where or for home [whom] I now not

I will get you what you want near my settlement if it should ^not be all taken up before I get out

I have hands now ingaged to work for me, and when I go out I shall Raise a Cabin and Clar som Land, on any Land I shall Like, or think will sute

---

1 All that portion of Pennsylvania west of the Alleghanies was then in possession of the Six Nations.

2 Chartier's.   3 Fort Pitt.

you — I shall take a sett of Survayers instruments and Pitch upon a begining, and run round the [w]hole and slash down som bushes taking the several Corses which will inable you the better to make the Entry

As to the Land in the Kings sid[e] of the Line, there has been but few setled there yeat or $_\wedge$at Least when I cam down, as they Line Runs farther south of Pittsburgh than was ever amagened, the Line Croses Cheet River at McCulecks Landing, about 5 miles from the mouth, they have Run as far as monongahalia, but is stop! there by the Endies ho [1] I understand says the shall not Run any farther till they are paid for the Land, which will put a stop to the Line? being Run till a Counsil is held, and they Result of that Known, but as to they Truth of it I Donot now, as it was only flying news, but I am Redy to think there may be som thing in it, as the Endiens are not pay? for the Land, The have told me that they cold not tell they Reason that Sir William Johnston Shold Ask them for Land to setle his poor People in, and then not pay them for it, nor alow they poor People, to setle on its som of them says they beleve som of the Great men in Philidelphia wants to take the Land them selves, but however be that as it will, it cannot be setled till the Line is Run, and then the Crown will know what Each has to pay the Endiens for, which would have bin done this fall if they are not stop!, There is no Liberty for setling in Pensilvania or that part soposed to be in Pens? yeat, but I beleve there would

---

[1] Indians who.

as soon as the Line was Run, they Line if Run out would go over Monongahalia about 30 Miles, and where the North $_\wedge$ will Cross Ohio I do not now till I see the end of the west Line, and then I can com midling near to it, but I am apt to think it will Cross below Fort Pitt, that I shall $_\wedge$ better able to satisfie you in my next Letter.[1]

---

[1] The boundary line between Pennsylvania and Maryland was surveyed by Charles Mason and Jeremiah Dixon, who came from England for that purpose. A few extracts from Mason's original journal may be of interest in showing the time involved (noting dates) in this then stupendous undertaking.

1763.
November 15th Arrived at Philadelphia.
Decembr 13th Got the Observatory finish'd, and fixed up our Instruments proper for observing

1764.
January 4th Finished our observations at Philadelphia.
11th The Observatory taken down and put with the rest of our Instruments into three wagons, except the Telescope &c of the Sector; which was carried on the Springs (with feather beds under it) of a Single Horse Chair.

1766
October 20 The Stones all Set; which finishd, the Tangent Line; From the Tangent Point to the West Line; and 65 Miles of the said West Line, or Boundary between Maryland and Pensylvania; The 64th Mile from the beginning of the West Line excepted, at which there is no Stone.
Novr 21 Attended the Gent: Commissioners. At this Meeting the Commrs agreed we should immediately proceed to extend the West Line (from the Post Mark'd West in Mr Bryans field) Eastward to the River Delaware. And also Resolved that Genl Johnson (his Majesties Agent for Indian Affairs) should be apply'd to (if they will not sell their Land) for to gain the Consent of the Six Nations to let us continue the West Line to the extent of the Provinces —

1767
June 3 Were informed that an agreement was concluded with the Six Nations for we to proceed with ye West Line —
July 8 At ye Allegany Mountain; where we left off last Summer.
October 9 Continued the Line to a High Ridge, At 231-20 Cross'd a War Path at Dunckard Creek . . . This day the Chief of the Indians which joyn'd us on ye 16th of July inform'd us that the above mentioned War Path, was the extent of his commission from the Chiefs of the Six Nations that he should go with us, with the Line; and that he would not proceed one step farther Westward. [The line was not extended farther until 1784.]

I com now to your next proposel in Regard to Looking out Land in the King part I shall heartily imbrass your Offer upon the Terms you proposed, and as soon as I get out, and my Afairs setled in _∧ to ^{Regard} the first Matter proposed, I shall set out in scharch of the Latter, as it may be don under a hunting sceem, which I intend befor you wrote me, and I had the same Sceem in my head but was _∧ a loss how to ^{at} Accomplish it, wanting a Person in home I cold confide, and one [w]hos[e] intrust cold answear my ends and there own, I have had serveral Offers, but have not agreed to any nor will I concearn with any but your self and home you think proper [1]

There will be a Large body of Land on the south side of the west Line towards the heads of Monongahilia waters, and head watters of Green briar and new [2] River but the Latter I am apt to think will be taken befor I can get to see it, as I understand there

---

December 26   Attended the Gent? Commissioners. When y⁰ Gent? Commissioners read their Minutes to us, by which we understand they have no farther occasion for us to run any more Lines for the Honble Proprietors, (but they did not chuse to give us a discharge in writing).

     1768

Septr. 11   At 11½ A M went on Board the Hallifax Packet Boat, for Falmouth — Thus ends my restless progress in America ———

C : MASON

[1] " I offered in my last to join you, in attempting to secure some of the most valuable lands in the Kings part, which I think may be accomplished after a while, notwithstanding the proclamation [of 1763], that restrains it at present, and prohibits the settling of them at all; for I can never look upon that proclamation in any other light (but this I say between ourselves) than as a temporary expedient to quiet the minds of the Indians. It must fall, of course, in a few years, especially when those Indians consent to our occupying the lands. Any person, therefore, who neglects the present opportunity of hunting out good lands, and in some measure marking and distinguishing them for his own, in order to keep others from settling them, will never regain it." — Washington to Crawford, September 21, 1767.

[2] Kanawha, which in the Indian language signifies " new."

has bin some Gentlemen that way this summer Doct Walker and som others but you can inform your self of there intentions

I shall Examine all the Creeks from the head of Monongahalia down to the Fort, and in the Forks of the River Ohio and New River, or as far as time wil allow me between this and Crismus, you may depend upon my Loosing no time, I will Let you know by all Oppertunitys What may hapen worthy your notis, and I should be glad of your advise by all oppertunitys

I think it would be adviseable to write to Col? Armstrong the First opertunity — I understand that he is one of the Survayers, and may have the office in Carlyle for all I [k]now, but I shall [k]now soon my self

You may depend upon my Keeping the hole as a profond secret,[1] and Trust the Searhing out the Land to my own Care which shall be done as soon as posable, and when I have Completed the hole I shall wait on you at your own house wheare I shall be able to give you a more satisfactory account of what I have Transacted ——

As to Nails and Comp[ys] [2] Grant it was Laid on the fork of Monongahalia and Yochagania which if Pen-

---

1 "I recommend, that you keep this whole matter a secret, or trust it only to those, in whom you can confide, and who can assist you in bringing it to bear by their discoveries of land. This advice proceeds from several very good reasons, and, in the first place because I might be censured for the opinion I have given in respect to the King's proclamation, and then, if the scheme I am now proposing to you were known, it might give the alarm to others, and, by putting them upon a plan of the same nature, before we could lay a proper foundation for success ourselves, set the different interests clashing, and, probably, in the end, overturn the whole." — Washington to Crawford, Sept. 21, 1767.

2 Neale and Company.

silvania taks its Charter will take it at any Rate, they Ohio Company you are the best Judge your self what will be done in it, or wheare it will be Lade[1] —

As I have a mind to Trade som with the Endiens and may be of advantage to me, in som Respect towards find[ing] out the best Land, as they Endiens is more oblidging to those ho Trade with them than others, and it would put me on an Equil footing with other Traders at fort pitt ho might want to take an advantage of me if I Trade without Lisences

Sir if it was not to much Trouble for you to procure them for me, if you would do it, it would greatly Oblidge me ——

As to the particqualars of what you wrote I cannot satisfie you better at Present than I have but Everything else you may Depend upon time and my own industry to Comply with as soon as in my power, **Sir** Excuse any Eror that I may have comited —

I am with Regard your very

NB there is nothing   Hum.[e] Sarvant
to be feared from the   W. CRAWFORD[2]
Maryland back Line
as it dos not go
over the Mountain[3]

---

[1] The Ohio Company possessed a grant of five hundred thousand acres of land in this vicinity; it was, however, never surveyed.

[2] Between the *Washington-Crawford Letters* (edited by C. W. Butterfield), including quotations from them used as notes elsewhere, and the present publication, there are some discrepancies, as The Colonial Dames are publishing *verbatim* copies of original letters.

[3] At this period, "the Maryland back line" was a subject of controversy between the provinces of Maryland and Virginia, depending upon the question of the location of the "first fountain of the Potomac," as the line was defined to be a meridian, extending from that point to the southern boundary line of Pennsylvania. The province of Virginia claimed all the territory west of the head of the *south* branch, while Maryland

FROM JOHN ARMSTRONG, ESQ.[1]

CARLISLE, 3.ᵈ Novemb.ʳ 1767 —

DEAR SIR

With particular pleasure I acknowledge the receit of your favour of the 21ˢᵗ Sept.ʳ but know not when it may meet with a Safe conveyance, I shall detain the letter a little, and if none appear, shall risque it by the way of Winchester or Phild.ᵃ

Your Information that part of the Lands on the Yaughyaughgheny & Monongahela formerly conceived to lie within the bounds of y.ʳ Governm.ᵗ is now likely to fall within the Limits of Pensylvania may I think prove very true; but that part of it that respects the making of Entries or issuing Grants at Carlisle, is entirely vauge & without foundation, that Office being alwaies restricted to Philadelphia & kept by the Proprietaries Secretary (at present James Tilghman Esq.ʳ) who in extraordinary Cases consults the Governor & Board of Property — wc.ʰ Board are only Assistants to the Governor he being Sole Commissioner of Property, nor is the Governor himself as yet by any means at Liberty to grant any Lands

insisted that her territory extended as far west as the head of the *north* branch. As in neither case would it be beyond "the mountain," Crawford could, with propriety, declare there was "nothing to be feared from it." — BUTTERFIELD.

1 Major-General John Armstrong was born in Ireland in 1720, and died at Carlisle, Pa., March 9, 1795. He emigrated to Pennsylvania between the years 1745 and 1748, and settled in the Kittatinny valley. He was by profession a surveyor, and in that capacity rendered many important services to the Colony. In 1756 he entered the military life as a private soldier, and steadily rose, until, on June 5, 1777, he was commissioned Major-General and Commander of the Pennsylvania troops. Previous to the Revolution he performed many important services in expeditions against the Indians. In November, 1778, he was elected a member of Congress. A fort erected at Kittanning in 1779 was named in his honor, and in 1800 a new county was designated Armstrong County. He was the father of General John Armstrong, Secretary of War under Madison.

beyond the Aleghany Mountains until they are first purchas'd of the Six Nation Indians which purchase has been on foot for some time past & its said will be concluded by Sir Wm Johnston this ensuing Spring or Summer, at which time 'tis _∧also said Sir W^m will make a Purchase on behalf of the Crown, of larger extent than the limits of Pensylvania, perhaps West of Virginia, but of this I have no certainty — so that_∧ at present Sir, you may firmly depend that nothing cou'd be farther attempted than a distant or conditional application to Governor Penn for a Tract or two on them Waters when the Purchase shall be confirm'd, which done in your Polite manner & under good pretentions too, I'm persuaded cou'd give no Offense, nor easily fail of Success — and if any Offices of mine either on the present or any other Occasion, may be of the least use I beg you wou'd freely command them, as they are now tendered and shall be chearfully employed as often as you shall give me leave. and perhaps on the first opportunity I have of going to Town I may take the Liberty of feeling his Hon^{rs} Pulse at least assist the foundation for any application you may afterwards think proper to make

As to the mode of taking up or having Lands granted in our Province, it has been considerably loose — the general intention of the Proprietaries has been a Competant Plantation of 2, or 300 acres to each Settler more especially since the Government became populous; but their Rule for various reasons has not been generally adher'd to, nor cou'd it well be, and however just in itself as a general

guide, has been much eluded especially of late when the Artifice of borrowing Names, or taking Out Warrants & Orders of Survey in the Names of other People as tho' they were for their use & afterward procuring conveyances from those whose names they had made use of, has so much prevail'd y.̇ many & not the most deserving has ingross'd large quantities. this occasion'd some noise among the populace, has made the Governor and Agents very uneasy & indeed prevents the moderate gratification of many deserving persons to whom some distinction is due; for the cry is that we shall have no strong Settlements backward because of those ingrossers. In locating of Lands we generally describe the Spot as nearly as we can, and the Surveys are expected to be made as regular as the nature of the Land will any ᴧway admit, that is by a four lin'd figure in order to prevent Culling, but our Mountanious Country Seldom admits a regular Survey, and the discretion of the Surveyor must take place.

As to the expence of our Proprietary Land the terms are now somewhat different from what they have been, £15„10.̇ Currency consideration Money ℔ hundred Acres & one halfpenny Sterling ℔ Acre ground Rent per Annum, has formerly been the price, but latterly they have fix'd the Consideration money per hundred Acres only at £5 Sterling & the yearly Quit Rent is rais'd to One penny Sterling ℔ Acre — what the Next purchase beyond the Mountains may be I cannot tell but immagin it will be on the terms last described above, as landed people seldom come down Stairs, and indeed there are so many

desirous of taking up lands, that they know very well that their terms will be comply'd with tho' so distant from trade & other conveniences of life. In regard to the line now running betwixt us and Mary-land — it will very probably be establish'd, but that in my opinion, must at least be pronounc'd by the Commissioners on each Side the question, or perhaps be confirm'd by the Partys on the other Side the Atlantick before it be a final boundary to these provinces, and how far y.ᵗ consideration may happen to retard the grant of Lands near yᵉ line may be questionable. I know a Certain Case depending near the line, where neither Province at present, seem willing to assume the Jurisdiction.[1] I'm sorry these Subjects had not happen'd to Occur when Hast the pleasure of seeing you — but here permit a ᴬSingle remark flowing from Old friendship, and it shall be on the infatuating Game of Card-playing, of which on thirty years observation I am not able to say so much good, as a witty person once did of what he Censur'd as a Culpable & extravagant piece of Dress *that it cover'd a multitude of Sins;* but that game always unfriendly to Society, turns conversation out of Doors, and curtails our opportu-

---

[1] Many perplexing questions arose at this time in consequence of the re-adjustment of the dividing line. William Edmiston wrote to Lord Baltimore in July, 1767: "In the year 1701 a large Quantity of Land was purchased of M.ʳ Penn by a Number of Adventurers, which was located to them in the Township of West Nottingham in the lower End of Chester County nearly adjoyning to what was then supposed to be the Boundary between the Provinces of Pennsylvania and Maryland; but as it appears by the late Settlement of the Line between the Two Provinces that great part of the Tract Purchased as afordsᵈ of M.ʳ Penn falls within the Province of Maryland my humble request is that I may obtain from my Lord Baltimore a Patent for such Part of the s.ᵈ Land as I now Inherit from my Father, who was one of the Original Purchasers and which is part of what falls into the Province of Maryland as aforesaid."

nities to mutual good. I can easily presume on
your good nature to forgive this piece of unfashiona-
ble freedom, and Believe _{me} to be with great respect —
Dear Sir

Your Most Obed.^t

And Most humb.^l Servt

P. S.   JOHN ARMSTRONG

Mrs Armstrong and
myself beg you'll please
to present our best respects
to your Lady & also to _{y.t} worthy
Neighbours, Coll. Fairfax & Lady.
we have both I hope been better'd
by the Warm Springs, except some
returns of the Rheumitism that
attend Mrs Armstrong, which I apprehend is so constitutional y.^t we
can scarcely expect a perfect cure.

J. A.

20th Decemb.^r

We have just rec.^d information that Genr.^l Gage has
wrote Governor Penn, that Sir Wm Johnson appre-
hends the Indians will break out this ensuing Spring
— and that the Generals letter is conceiv'd in such
terms as has mov'd the Governor to advise in Council whether the Assembly shou'd be call'd; but as
they Sit early in Janr.^y the Governor has not issu'd
a Summons — May God avert such a Calamitous
Scene, for shou'd it happen a third time so near together, Our Frontier People appear to be undone.
Capt Callendor has very lately rec.^d a letter from a

Trader at y.ᵉ lower Shawna Town, who says that
them Indians are at present very quiet, but express
some fears of your Government 'tis also said that
M.ʳ Croghan has lately had an amicable interview w.ᵗʰ
various Tribes at Detroit. these last appear to be
ags.ᵗ Sir W.ᵐˢ Intelligence.[1]

FROM CAPTAIN ROBERT STEWART.

My Dear Sir

In my last from London I gave you a detail of the
various schemes I had form'd and of the great disappointments I had experienced in endeavouring to
carry them into execution, I was at length appointed
Comptroller of his Majesty's Customs in this place,
an Office which I was inform'd was a very reputable
one and worth at least a thousand Sterling ℔ ann :
the first part of the information I found Just, but I
have the mortification to find that the value of my
Office is by the opening the free Ports in this Island
and by some late regulations in the Revenues dimin-
ished near a half : however even what I enjoy would
in some Countries do very well for a Batchelor in my
way but in this extravagant and very expensive place
where all the necessaries and most of the conven-

---

1 In 1767–68, another savage war menaced the colonists on account of the dissatisfaction of the Indians in regard to the encroachments on their lands. At Sir William
Johnson's suggestion, a great council was held at Fort Stanwix in the latter part of
October, 1768, at which over two thousand Indians were present, besides the govern-
ors of several of the colonies. A treaty was here concluded on November 5, in which
the Six Nations relinquished their claim to all the land within a boundary extending
from near Lake Ontario, at the junction of Canada and Wood Creeks, to Owego on
the Susquehanna, thence through Pennsylvania, Maryland, etc., to the mouth of the
Tennessee. This was called the New Purchase.

iencies of Life are exorbitantly dear, it is barely sufficient to support me in a decent manner. I likewise
informed you that your old Acquaintance and my
very good Friend M.̇ Macleane had directed me to
desire you would Draw upon him at sixty days sight
for the amount of the money you was generously
pleas'd in the handsomest and most Friendly manner
to advance to me, before I left N. America, for which
and your invariable and polite attention to my welfare my heart will never cease to glow with the most
lively ardour of the strongest Friendship and genuine gratitude, and allow me My dear Col to assure
you with sacred truth that few things could yield
me more pleasure than opportunities of evincing
that these are the sincere sentiments of a heart that
will ever love and esteem you, I likewise desired that
you would please address your Bills for that Sum to
Lauchlin Macleane Esq.̇ in Queen ann Street, Cav-
endish-Square London.

A few days after date of my last I embarked in the
Ship Trent Cap.̇ Gillis and had a Passage of 14 weeks
from Gravesend — our very tedious Passage was rendered doubly disagreeable, whilst in Northern Cli-
mates by a great deal of bad weather and on our getting
to the South.̇ by Calms not less alarming from the
dreadfull consequences a continuance of them would
inevitably have produced — We stopt near two weeks
at Madeira, an African Island peopled by and under
the Dominion of Portugal, that Island is well known
by its excellent Wines is in a most delightfull Climate where extremes of heat and cold are never felt,
it is covered with an eternal verdure which runs up

even to the summit of its immense high Mountains, which branch out into a variety of odd Figures that form many Vallies now converted into rich Vineyards which produce no less than twenty three different species of Grapes from which nineteen thousand Pipes of wine are annually made — Citrons, Lemons, Oranges, Aples, Peaches and in short most of the Tropical and European Fruits grow there to perfection — Its principal Town Fench Hall[1] stretches along a spacious Bay nearly in the form of a Crescent it is defended by a number of Forts & Batteries which the Portuguese think very formidable but in reality they are but trifling it contains near twenty thousand Inhabitants the whole number in the Island is eighty thousand Blacks included Their houses are quite white in the outside, in Town as well as on the many Plantations on the Face of the Mountains, the whole yields a prospect perfectly Romantic and as charming as the imagination can well conceive — The British Factory chiefly composed of Scotch are about thirty Families and Live in the utmost harmony and socibility, they have Card and Dancing Assemblies, Parties to the Country, and they participate of every amusement that retired Mountanious place will admit of, By their frequent excursions to the Country and an emulation to excell, the Ladies ride their little Horses and Mules with a spirit and tranquility, precipes that the very sight of would strike an American or English Lady with terror, and amazement. The Portuguese Ladies do not associate with our Ladies nor even with their own Gentle-

---

1 Funchal.

men, their Churches which are open every day are
the only public places at which their rigorrious Customs permits them to appear, thither I sometimes
went to gratify my curiosity and tho' they were generally filled, chiefly by Females, I did not see one
fine Woman amongst them, some of them are tolerably genteel, severals have good Eyes and Teeth and
they in general have very fine hair which they dress
in a taste peculiarly pleasing — A few days before I
left that Island a man of war arrived from Lisbon
with a new Governor, all the Men in the Island were
ordered under Arms to receive him, they cut but an
indifferent Figure and made very awkward regular
Fires both from their Artillery and Musketry; The
Gov.ʳ went immediately to the principal Fort, and
his Lady to Church, she appears not above fifteen,
was drest in a man's hat fiercely Cocked with a
broad Gold Lace and her hair in a Bag with a Solli-
taire, she was attended with an English and French
Lady — The next day the old Govern.ʳ embarked ; a
venerable looking man, he was double the usual time
Gov.ʳ and went off poor, nor did he live splendidly
but employed all his Money in acts of charity and
humanity, he was attended to the waterside by all

---

1 The Heirs of Wᵐ Strother Gentⁿ decᵈ . . . Dʳ

July 19 1756	To Cash paid Mʳ Anthony Strother by Colˢ Fieldˢ Lewis, for Land bought of your Estate and recovered from him by Colˢ Henry Fitzhugh . . .ᵂ	£43 .. 10 .. 9
		£43 .. 10 .. 9
1770 Janʸ 1	To Ball. pʳ Contra	22 .. 16 .. 3
1772 Jan-1	To Ballˢ foᵣm Ledger A	£22 .. 16 .. 3

FROM MR. GABRIEL JONES.

DEAR SIR

I acknowledged the receipt of yours of 25th February & recommended it to ye care of Col^o F. Lewis in hopes it might ~~call~~ ^{meet you} in your way to ye Assembly in March, but whether it did I have not as yet learned & least a miscarriage should have happened, I write this to inform you of my acquainting Messrs Lewis & Madison with your proposal of paying what you had advanced for ye deficiency of ye Land purchased from Mr Strother Executor, they as well as my self do readily agree to advance our proportionable parts as soon as you let me know what it is —

I am with much esteem & respect Dr Sir

Y^r most Obed^t ~~hble~~ Servt

May 3^d 1768
Winchester

GABRIEL JONES

FROM COLONEL THOMAS MOORE.

DEAR SIR

I am very sorry to fine the meathod I took to prevent your loosing any interest on the money I owe was not agreeable to you but as I am resolved not a farthing shall be lost for your kind indulgence to me I am willing to do any thing in my power you may think right   If you think proper to let the Bond lay as it is till next Octr Court you may then depend on great part of the money if not the whole and at any rate no interest shall be lost but if this way should not be agreable pray direct me and depend on my

doing any thing in my power to comply with your desire — As my money will not be due till the Oct.ʳ Court it will not be in my power to pay it sooner & therefore hope you will not run me to the Charge of a Suit, which will not answer any satisfactory end —

I am with my best complements to your Lady & with distinguished regard to your self Dear Sir

Your Ob.ᵗ hble Se.ᵗ

May 12. 1768   Thoˢ Moore

FROM THE REV. JONATHAN BOUCHER.[1]

Caroline, June 13ᵗʰ 1768.

Sir

I think myself much obliged to You for the flattering Preference given Me, in thinking Me a proper person to undertake the Direction of Master Custis's Education. And I will not hesitate to confess to You, that it wou'd mortify Me not a little to be deprived of so acceptable an Opportunity of obtaining some Credit to myself: which I flatter myself there wou'd be no Danger of, from so promising a Youth. — Yet I am under a Necessity of informing You of a Circumstance in my affairs which may prob-

---

1 Jonathan Boucher was born in England, March 12, 1738. In early youth he came to America as tutor to the sons of a Virginia planter, and in 1762 entered the Anglican ministry. He seems, however, to have had an especial fondness for his early profession, as he continued to practice it after taking orders, and carried on a boarding-school of from thirty to forty boys. John Parke Custis became his pupil in 1768, at fourteen years of age, and remained under his charge for several years. Dr. Boucher was an avowed loyalist, and so offensive were his tenets to the colonists that in 1775 he was obliged to return to England, where he was appointed vicar of Epsom. He died there April 27, 1804.

ably lead You to look out for another Tutor for your Ward. — Preferments in the Church in Virginia are so extremely scanty, that I have for some time been endeavouring to establish an Interest in Maryland, where, I doubt not but You know, the Livings are much better. I happened to be in Annapolis, chiefly upon this Business, at the Time your Letter reach'd this Place : and tho' I have already met with two Disappointments, yet, I have received fresh Promises that I shall now soon be provided for. If This happens at all, as I have all ye Reason in ye World to believe that it will, the Parish I expect is That of Annap^s, where also I propose to continue superintending the Education of a few Boys.

Now, Sir, it will be necessary for You to consider, whether in Case such a Change sh^d take Place, it w^d be agreeable to You that Mast^r Custis shou'd accompany Me thither : for, otherwise I can hardly suppose You will think it worth his While to come down hither, probably, for a few Months only. For my Part, I cannot help imagining that You will think Annap^s a more eligible Situation, as it is, I believe, rather more convenient to You, & a Post Town from whence You might have Letters, if necessary, every Week to Alexandria. But This is a matter on which You alone ought to judge, & in which perhaps it becomes not Me to give my Opinion. All I have to add, is, that sh^d You resolve, at all Events, to trust the young Gentleman to my Care, either Here or in Maryland, I will exert my best Endeavours to render him worthy of Yours, & his Family's Expectations. And as He is now, as You justly observe, losing

Time, wou'd it be amiss to send Him down immediately, if it were only upon Tryal, as I presume He has never yet been remov'd from under the Wing of his Parents: You will then, from his own Reports of Me, & my Management of my Pupils, be better able to judge of the Propriety of continuing ₍Him₎ with Me. And tho' it be usual for Boys to find their own Beds, in this Case, that wou'd be unnecessary: I will furnish Him for the little Time He will have to stay before I know what my Destiny is to be. As to Terms &c, these may be settted hereafter: all I shall now say of Them is, that, from what I have heard of Coll? Washington's Character, They are such as I am well convinc'd He will not think unreasonable.

I have been under much Concern that it was not sooner in my Power to acknowledge the Rec: of y: obliging Letter: this is forwarded by a Serv: of M: Addison's, whom I have requested to send it over to Alexandria, by w? means I hope You will receive it sooner than by Post.

I am, very respectfully, Sir,
Y: most Obedient, &
most Hble Serv:
JONA: BOUCHER

FROM THE REVEREND JONATHAN BOUCHER.

SIR

Altho' I have already return'd an Answ: to y: obliging Letter of the 30ᵗʰ Ult: by a Serv: of the Rev: M: Addison's who went from hence a Day or two

ago, yet as You seem'd desirous to hear from Me as soon as possible, & as Coll.° Lewis now informs Me that He can furnish Me with an Opp.ᵗʸ directly to your House, I am desirous to convince You, that I have not been inattentive to the Matter of y.ʳ Request. In my former L.ʳ, I have inform'd You of my Expectations of removing shortly to Annap.ˢ, where I propose also to continue to take Care of a few Boys, & have left it to Y.ʳself to judge whether, in that Case, it wou'd be agreeable to You & M.ʳˢ Washington, that Mast.ʳ Custis sh.ᵈ accompany Me thither, as, unless He shou'd, I imagin'd You wou'd hardly think it worth while to send Him abroad to a School, w.ᶜ may probably be broke up in a very few Months. I added also, that sh.ᵈ You approve of This, I shou'd be glad He might come down hither, in the manner You have propos'd, immediately; which, I suppose, He may easily do, as there will be no Occasion for his making much Preparation; since, if I sh.ᵈ be so unfortunate as to be again disappointed in Maryland, & be obliged to remain still where I now am, it will be as easy for You hereafter to furnish Him w.ᵗʰ any thing He may happen to want: and in the mean Time, it will be no Inconvenience to Me to let Him use one of my Beds &c — And This is all, or nearly all, I yet have it in my Power to give You for Ans.ʳ: I sincerely wish the Uncertainty of my present Prospects wou'd allow Me to speak more positively.

Ever since I have heard of Mast.ʳ Custis, I have wish'd to call Him one of my little Flock; and I am not asham'd to confess to You, that, since the Rec.ᵗ of y.ʳ Letter, I have wish'd it much more. Engag'd as

I have now been for upwards of seven Years in the Education of Youth, You will own it must be mortifying to Me to reflect, that I cannot boast of having had the Hon.ʳ to bring up one Scholar. I have had, 'tis true, Youths, whose Fortunes, Inclinations & Capacities all gave Me Room for yᵉ most pleasing Hopes: yet I know not how it is, no sooner do They arrive at that Period of Life when They might be expected more successfully to apply to their Studies, than They either marry, or are remov'd from School on some, perhaps even still, less justifiable Motive. You, S.ʳ however, seem so justly sensible of yᵉ vast Importance of a good Education that I cannot doubt of your heartily concurring in every Plan that might be propos'd for yᵉ Advantage of y.ʳ Ward: And what I am more particularly pleased with; is, the ardent Desire You express for yᵉ Cultiva.ⁿ of his moral, as well as his intellectual Powers, I mean that He may be made a Good, as well as ₐlearned & a sensible Man. That Mast.ʳ Custis may be both, is the Sincere Wish of

Sir,

Y.ʳ most Obed.ᵗ &

CAROLINE ⎱
June 16ᵗʰ ⎰
1768

most H̶b̶l̶e̶ Serv.ᵗ

JONA.ᴺ BOUCHER

FROM WILLIAM SAVAGE, ESQ.

DUMFRIES 3.ᵈ July 1768 —

SIR

I rec.ᵈ y.ʳ favor of the 28ᵗʰ June, which I showed to M.ʳˢ Savage, after some little consideration she again

repeatedly assured me that as her desire to revoke
the Bond was perfectly voluntary, that she wou'd
take every method which you & M[r] Fairfax cou'd
possibly desire to convince you both that it was
so & also make you perfectly secure in Joining her
to relinquish the Bond — It gives me some uneasiness for fear you shou'd think that I am in the least
Urgent in this affair — But this uneasiness is much
lessened ~~upon~~ ᶦⁿ my full satisfaction that you w[d] find
upon the strictest Enquiry that this is quite a Voluntary step in M[rs] Savage, with these sentiments I
think Sir I might stand excused in avoiding payment
particularly as M[rs] Savage has in as effectual a manner as she cou'd without the concurrence of her
Trustees revoked her Right — But when I reflect
that it is very unreasonable that either You or M[r]
Fairfax shoud receive the least trouble that cou'd be
avoided in a Trust which you both have undertaken
to serve M[rs] Savage, ~~I am almost decided~~ & that
whatever Reason's you may have against Joining
her Revocation of the Bond must be also to serve
her I am almost induced to forego any immediate
advantage & [obliterated] offer any inconvency. that
may attend the Refusal of Her Voluntary offer —
But still I flatter myself that you & M[r] Fairfax will
upon further Reflection think with me (& in this case
~~I think~~ I think I have perfectly devested myself of
any kind of prejudice in Judging of it) that when
the Person for whose sole Benefit & Advantage a
Trust was Created has a desire to Renounce or Revoke the same that it is to be Reasonably expected

the Trustees can have no sort of objection — In the mean time I acknowledge the Justness of the demand of £100 payable last January & shall take some speedy opportunity to make payment   I am

Sir very Respectfully

Y^r most obed^t Servt

W^M SAVAGE

FROM THE REVEREND JONATHAN BOUCHER.

CAROLINE, July 15th 1768

DEAR SIR,

I have just Time to put a Cover over The Inclosed, and to add to the Informa^{ns} I suppose Mas^{tr} Custis himself has given You, that He has enjoyed perfect Health ever since You left Him, except^g two or three Days that He complained of a Pain in his Stomach, which I at first took for the Cholic, but since think it more likely that it might be owing to Worms.   As it easily went off, by two or three Medicines I gave Him, and as He has had no Returns, I did not think it necessary to consult Dr Mercer; which however I shall immediately do, if You desire it.

You will oblige Us by looking into y^r Books for a Work of Cicero's, De officies, or his Familiar Epistles. & [mutilated] Livy: & sending Them down by ye first Opportunity that offers.

Be so obliging to Me as to excuse the shortness of this Letter, it shall not be Long, ere I will write to

You more fully — The Messenger, who is to carry
This to y.ᵉ office now waits for Me.

      I am, very respectfully

           Y.ʳ most Obed.ᵗ Hble Serv.ᵗ

                    Jona.ᴺ Boucher

FROM BRYAN FAIRFAX, ESQ.

                 Alexandria July the 20ᵗʰ 1768 —

Dear Sir

    I have received your favor of the 20ᵗʰ and am
the more confirmed in the Opinion I had of Doctor
Savage's being fully persuaded that his Wife really
& sincerely desires the Relinquishment of the Bond,
and therefore am not ₍at₎ all surprised that he should in
such case desire it also. The Week before the last
she sent to me desiring that I would make a demand
for the money, and also that I would ~~make~~ meet her
at Greenhill, and by the return of the Messenger I
wrote to M.ʳ Savage & in plain terms told him that
his Wife was averse to the giving up the Bond, and
that I informed him of it to save him any further
trouble about it, and ₍yᵗ₎ I might not be under any
Necessity of giving another Refusal; at the same
time making a Demand for the Money due. When
I met her on Thursday last she shewed me my Letter to the D.ʳ and told me it had given her vast uneasiness, and gave me to understand that she was
notwithstanding to ask me again for the Bond at
that meeting; which must certainly in my opinion
be her own proposal to him. I told her I wished the

Bond was given up, being heartily tired of it, and
again begged of her to be frank & candidly own her
Sentiments, which she seemed to promise; but ~~in~~
the manner in which she proposed to declare her
Sentiments, convinces me that she will not own her
real Inclination, and moreover makes me doubtful
whether she will not deny that she ever expressed
her Desire to keep the Bond — I see nothing to
blame in him about it, for it is very reasonable
that he should join with her Desire to obtain it, but
from some circumstances I am apt to think he looks
upon me as interested, and for that reason if you
have no Objection I should be glad if you would also
satisfie him with regard to her real Inclination that
we may be no more plagued about it. Upon proviso
however that you believe with me that she is in no
fear of her Life, which is the only thing which can
excuse her present Conduct.

I shall be very glad of your Company at Towlston
when it is convenient to spend three or four days or
more — I can't say my hounds are good enough to
justifie an Invitation to hunt, but out of that Regard
I have always entertained & which I perceive en-
creases with Time I shall be extremely glad of your
Company and we may then partake of that diversion
or not as it may seem agreeable; in the former Case
a change of dress would be very necessary. I shall
be at home from the 1st of August 'till our Court
except the Monday & tuesday of Loudon Court, and
if in that time it should be convenient & you should
have an Opportunity of seeing Doctor Romney or

any other you choose to attend you No one will be
more proud of your Company than

sir Y.^r most obed.^t Servt

BRYAN FAIRFAX.

FROM BRYAN FAIRFAX, ESQ.

TOWLSTON July the 30.th 1768 —

DEAR SIR

Since I wrote to you last I have _∧a Letter from D.^r
Savage wherein he says that his Wife acknowledges
that she had once in a discontented Mood expressed
a Dislike to parting with the Bond, but that she had
fully convinced me at our last meeting of her earnest
desire to relinquish it: At the same time Mrs Savage
also wrote to me begging a thousand pardons of you
& me for the trouble she had given us, and mentions
her Intention of going to Ireland immediately, and
desires the Bond may be given up. I am to acknowledge your favor of the 25.th and entirely agree with
you in Sentiments — I have thought proper to mention the contents of the two last Letters, tho' I don't
know that it can make any Alteration in our proceedings to obtain the Sum due.

I remain

Dr Sir

Your most obed.^t Servt

BRYAN FAIRFAX.

FROM THE REVEREND JONATHAN BOUCHER.

S.^t M<small>ARY</small>'<small>S</small> August 2.^d 1768.

S<small>IR</small>

I do not recollect that Mast.^r Custis has had any Return of ye Pain in his Stomach which I told You I suspected to be occasioned by Worms: but as it is but too probable that He may have a little of the Ague & Fever in This or ye next Month, this Complaint, it is not unlikely, may return; and if it does, in any considerable degree, Dr Mercer shall be consulted.

Mast.^r Custis is a Boy of so exceedingly mild & meek a Temper, that I meant no more by my Fears, than a Doubt that possibly He might be made uneasy by ye rougher Manners of some of his School fellows. I am pleas'd, however, to find that He seems to be perfectly easy & happy in his new Situation; and as the first Shock is now over, I doubt not but He will continue so. You know how much the Question has been agitated between ye Advantages of a private & a public Educat.ⁿ: & this young G–man has afforded Me Occasion to reflect upon it rather more than I had done before. His Educat.ⁿ hitherto may be call'd a private one; & to This perhaps chiefly, He owes that peculiar Innocence & *Sanctity of Manners* w.^c are so amiable in Him: but then, is He not, think You, more artless, more unskill'd in a necessary Address, than He ought to be, 'ere He is turned out into a World like This? In a private Seminary his Passions cou'd be seldom aroused: He had few or no Competitors, and therefore cou'd not so advantageously, as in a more public

Place, be inured to combat those little oppositions & Collisions of Interest, w.ᶜ resemble in Miniature the Contests y.ᵗ happen in y.ᵉ gr.ᵗ School of y.ᵉ World. And let our Circumstances in y.ᵉ World be what They will, yet, considering the thousand unavoidable Troubles that human Nature is Heir to, This is a part of Educat.ⁿ tho' seldom attended to, w.ᶜ I think of more Importance than almost all y.ᵉ Rest. When Children are taught betimes to bear Misfortunes & cross Accidents w.ᵗʰ becom.ᵍ Fortitude, one half of y.ᵉ Evils of Life, w.ᵗʰ w.ᶜ others are dejected, afflict not Them. Educat.ⁿ is too generally considered merely as y.ʳ Acquisi.ⁿ of Knowledge, & y.ᵉ Cultiva.ⁿ of y.ᵉ intellectual Powers: And agreeably to this Notion, w.ⁿ We speak of a Man well-educated, We seldom mean more than that He has been well instructed in those Languages w.ᶜ are y.ᵉ Avenues to Knowledge. But surely, this is but a partial & imperfect Acc.ᵗ of it: & y.ᵉ Aim of Educat.ⁿ sh.ᵈ be not only to form wise but good Men, not only to cultivate y.ᵉ Understanding, but to expand y.ᵉ Heart, to meliorate y.ᵉ Temper, & *fix y.ᵉ gen'rous Purpose in y.ᵉ glowing Breast.* But whether This can best be Done, in a private or public School, is a Point, on w.ᶜ so much may be said on both Sides, that I confess myself still undetermined. Y.ʳ Son came to Me teeming w.ᵗʰ all y.ᵉ softer Virtues: but then I thought, possess'd as He was of all y.ᵉ Harmlessness of y.ᵉ Dove, He still wanted some of y.ᵉ Wisdom of y.ᵉ Serpent: And This, by y.ᵉ Oeconomy of my Family he will undoubtedly sooner acquire than at Home. But ~~then,~~ how will You forgive Me sh.ᵈ I suffer Him to lose in Gentleness, Simplicity, & Inoffensiveness, as much as He gains in Address,

Prudence, & Resolu^n.? And I must assure You f^m Experience, that This is a Dilemma by no means so Easily avoided in Practice, as it may seem to be in Theory. Upon the Whole, however, I can honestly give it as my Opinion, (& as it must give You & Mrs Washington much comfort & Pleasure to hear it I hope You will not suspect y^t I w^d be so mean as to say so, if I did not think so) that I have not seen a Youth that I think promises fairer to be a good & useful Man than John Custis! 'Tis true, he is far f^m being a brilliant Genius, but This so far from being considered as a Reflection upon Him, ought rather to give You pleasure. Parents are gen-

erally $_\wedge$ to gr^t Vivacity & Sprightliness of Genius in

^{partial}

th^r Children; whereas I think, that there cannot be a Symptom less expressive of future Judgement & Solidity: as it seems thoroughly to preclude not only Depth of Penetra^n, but y^t Atten^n. & Applica^n w^c are so essentially requisite in ye Acquisi^n of Knowledge. It is, if I may use ye Simile of a Poet, a busy Bee, whose whole Time passes away in mere Flight f^m Flower to Flower, with^t rest^s upon Any a suff^t Time to gather Honey.

He will Himself inform You of ye Accident He lately met with; and as He seems to be very appre-hensive of y^r Displeasure, c^d I suppose it necessary, I w^d urge You & his Mamma to spare Rebukes, as much as He certainly deserves Them. Mrs Washington may believe Me that He is now perfectly well. He seemed to expect Me to employ a Doct^r, but as He met wth ye Accident by his own indiscre^n, & as I saw there was no Danger, I thought it not amiss not

to indulge Him. The calling in a Physician upon every trifling Occasion, I think, is too likely to render Children needlessly timorous & Cowardly.

I did not misunderstand ye Meaning of y^r Request,[1] in ye Matter wherein You suspect I possibly might; being persuaded that You know as well as I do, that such p^{r}ticular Attention is not only unnecessary, but impracticable. He will probably inherit a much more considerable Fortune, than any other Boy here; and I thought it by no means an improper or unreasonable Request that a p^{r}ticular Atten^n sh^d be bestowed on a Youth of his Expecta^n. But as any Partiality to Him in ye trifling Circumstances of his Diet, or other Accommoda^{ns} w^d be rather disservicable than otherwise, I have taught Him not to expect it. The only p^{r}ticular Atten^n You c^d wish for, I also think Him entitled to; & that is, a more vigilant Atten^n to ye Propriety & Decorum of his Behav^r, & ye restrain^g Him f^m many Indulgences, w^c I sh^d willingly allow p^{r}haps to ano^r Boy, whose Prospects in Life do not require such exalted Sentem^{ts} y^t allow^g Him more frequently to sit in my Company, & being more careful of ye Company of Those, who might probably debase or taint his Morals. — Had I my Choice, believe me, it w^d be more agreeable to Me to superintend ye Educat^n of two or three promis^g Lads, than to lead a Life of ye most voluptuous Indolence: but the Truth is, oblig'd as I was to engage in it by Necessity, & not by Choice, I have often found myself so ill requited, & ye office itself considered as so

---

[1] That Doctor Boucher might give to his (Washington's) ward a "peculiar care," "as he is a promising boy, the last of his family, and will inherit a large fortune."

low, & so often taken up by yᵉ very lowest Fellows one knows of, that after having laboured in it for upwards of seven Years, withᵗ havᵍ added much either to my Fortune or Reputation, I am almost resolv'd to drop it entirely.   Yet, whilst it continues to be agreeable to You to let Mastʳ Custis remain wᵗʰ Me, it will be a Pleasure to Me to have yᵉ Managemᵗ of Him, nor can I indeed come to any decisive Resoluⁿ as to yᵉ other Matter, till I know more certainly yᵉ Fate of my Expectaⁿˢ in Maryland.

Be so obliging as to find some speedy & safe Conveyance for a Lʳ to Mʳ Addison, wᶜ I take yᵉ Liberty of recommendᵍ to yʳ pʳticular Care, as it might be of much Detriment to Me, shᵈ it fall into ill Hands as has been yᵉ Case once before.

I beg Pardon for this very tedious Letter, wᶜ I have taxed You wᵗʰ yᵉ Perusal of, and, wᵗʰ Mine & my Sister's Compᵗˢ to Mʳˢ Washington

> I am, Sʳ
> Yʳ most Obedᵗ & most
> Hble Servᵗ
> JONAᴺ BOUCHER.

FROM THE REVEREND JONATHAN BOUCHER.

Dᴿ SIR

I am much concern'd for Mastʳ Custis's Indisposition, wᶜ yet I foresaw, & shᵈ have told You so, as I did Him, had I not been unwell at yᵉ Time He left Us.   He is fond of Fruit, &, wᵗ is worse for Him, He is fond of Cucumbers; & to These, I doubt not, in a grᵗ Measure, He owes his bilious Complaints.

A better Air, & stricter Attention, I trust, will soon restore Him to his former Health.

I did intend to have dismiss'd my Boys a Week ago; but th.r Parents & Friends hav.g neglected to send for Them, Many of Them have had, & still have this vile Disorder. And both my Sister & Usher are also down in it, I see no Chance I have of quitting y.e Place dur.g y.e sickly Season, w.c was my chief aim. Thank God, the Fevers are not very obstinate this Year, & easily give Way to Vomits & Bark.

Unless You hear from Me again, I shall be glad to see Jack here ag.n ab.t y.e latter End of this Month, if his Health will then permit Him: & I hardly expect He will be in a Capacity to leave Home much sooner. Then, I hope, He may come without Danger. M.r Addison is expected here every Day, who will probably either come or return Your Way.

I beg my Comp.ts to M.rs Washington, & her Son, & am

Y.r most obed.t Hble Serv.t

JONA.N BOUCHER

CAROLINE
Sep.t 5.th }
1768 }

FROM CAPTAIN WILLIAM CRAWFORD.

SPRINGGARDIN [1] Jan.y 7.th 1769

D.R SIR /

By V Crawford [2] Receved your Letter dated Nov.r 13th and inclosed twenty pounds Pensilvania mony

---

[1] Spring Garden was one of the names by which Crawford designated his home upon the Youghiogheny. — BUTTERFIELD.

[2] Valentine Crawford, brother of William.

I wrot you ^by^ Mr Harison,[1] he told me he gave Mrs Washington my Letter but you was not at home

At my Return from Fredrick over the mountain, the Survayor was Runing Land out for such as was Redy to pay him, Emedatly I got him to Run out your Land, have done it as if for my self taking all the good Land and Leveing all that was sory only som Joyning the Mill Seat

It came out in Locations as other Land — but was all Run out in one body but the survayor will be paid for Every 300 Acres notwith standing he run the hole in one body, he says it is the Rule of the Office, there is in Each Survay 332 and 333 Acres so I had good Meashure.

The Land you was to have of My Brother John Stephenson[2] when the survayor come was Located, he Lost all that is good without he can Purches the man's Right which he intends to do if he can, but I dout it as People from Pensilvania hold Land High You mentioned the Lins of the Colonys being Extended soon or at Least such a plan was on foot and that they officers would Obtain there Lands Agreeable to his Majesties Proclamation.[3]

I am at a Looss where they will Lay it of[f] as they Land to the Southard of Penns Line is very Sory Except in som spots unlass it is Layd of as you in a Letter before wrot me

I have not bin Down on any Part of the Little

---

1 Lawrence Harrison, Captain Crawford's son-in-law.

2 A half-brother of Crawford.   He had five half-brothers, sons of Richard Stephenson: John, Hugh, Richard, James, and Marcus. — BUTTERFIELD.

8 Of 1763. See Hening, vol. vii. p. 666.

Conaway[1] but has Conversed with Numbers that has bin from from the head to the Mouth ho tells me there is no Large bodys of Good Land on it is Chiefly mountains and brooken Land with hear and there a peace of very good Land.

In a few days I intend of Monongahalia to Run out som Land there which Draft I shall bring Down with [me] to your house About the first of Feb.̲ or Midle, I should have gone before but was stop.̲t by the Road as I had it to finish

I have found out a peace or two More of good Land in Pens Line which you may have I have taken them good for you, if you Chuse them I cold have taken more if I had thought they Quitrents would have bin Lesend as it is from a pany to a half pany an Acre

As soon as I return from ~~down~~ ^up^ the River I am to go over Monongahalia to Look at som Land two men has found on a Creek Call.̲d Ten Mile Creek and if I Like the Land you shall have any of it you may Like I shall be better able to satisfie you when I see you Sir I am your most Hum.̲l Sarv.̲t

W Crawford

N B by the Commanding Officer at Fort pitt there is a Negro woman sent me ho was taken[2] from a place Call.̲d Drapers Medows then they property of one Maj.̲r Winston ho is since Dead there was at first 22 taken in all from him but sevaral got away and got to there Master again

---

[1] Kanawha.
[2] By the Indians during Pontiac's war of 1763–64?

I understand the Colony paid for them if so she now belongs to the Colony[1]

If it is not to much Trouble for you I should be oblidged to you to inquire and find out the Truth of the Matter and you _{to} Purches her of the Colony for me Provided they would wait any time for the money it would be doing me a great favour

There is three more I belive I can get from the Nation[2] with som Trouble, they wench I have Run away from them & Cam to Fort pitt

I am afraid there is som on the scent [of] bying her alredy

WC——

FROM THE REVEREND JONATHAN BOUCHER.

DEAR SIR

I have been much concerned that it has not been in my Power to spend a few Days at Mount Vernon, as I hop'd I should. A very painful Disorder I labour'd under when Mast.[r] Custis left Me, confin'd Me to my Bed a Fortnight, and now it is too late to set out, when I expect all my little Flock to return immediately, as Some of Them already are. You will please therefore to let Mast.[r] Custis know, that it will be to no Purpose for Him now to wait for Me, as We proposed when We parted; & that I shall expect to see Him at S.[t] Mary's as soon as ever a good Day or two may tempt Him to set out.

---

[1] Virginia. [2] Six Nations.

If Mr Magowan be still with You, be so good as to enquire, if He rec.^d a L.^r f.^m Me ab.^t a Month ago : The Parish in Louisa I mentioned to Him is still vacant, tho' warmly sollicited for by his Fellow Candidate Mr Coutts, & others.

I am, very respectfully,

Y.^r most Obed.^t Hble serv.^t

FREDERICKSB.^G ⎱   JONA.^N BOUCHER
11.th Jany 1769 ⎰

FROM CAPTAIN ROBERT STEWART.

KINGSTON IN JAMAICA Jany 25.th 1769

MY DEAR COL.^O

I was some weeks out of Town for the benefit of my Health, which I seldom enjoy here, on my return to this place I had the immense pleasure to receive both your Affectionate and most acceptable Favors of the 5.th August via Barbados and of the 1.st Novem.^r under Cover from my Friend Mr Jameison from Norfolk, breathing those Sentiments of real Friendship which I have on all occasions had the happiness to experience by which I think myself greatly hon.^d and which I will ever deem one of the most happy and valueable acquisitions I made in Life, the kind manner in which you are pleased to enter into my present situation and the fears you apprehend on my acco.^t from the nature of this Climate at once evince the warmth of your regard and the rectitude of your opinion, which from a great variety of instances in the course of that agreeable part of my Life in which I had the honor and very great satisfaction to Serve

under your Orders I ever found supported by those powerfull reasons that are the certain marks of real Genius and a solid Judgement which seldom unite in one person; The Physician who I have chiefly employ'd in this Island (where I in general have been Sick and at best rather enjoy the absence of pain than good Health) has given it as his opinion that a perfect Recovery from my Bilious Disorder with which I am so much afflicted is not to be hoped for but in a Cold Climate, I have therefore resolved to embark for England the first good oppor.ᵞ after the vernal Equinox and tho my Constitution is much injured I have hopes given me that my native air exercise and a proper Regimen will in time effect the re : establishment of my Health, the deprivation of which in a great measure destroys the relish of most other enjoym.ᵗˢ you see by my dwelling so long upon this disagreeable Subject how much an Invalid I am — I sometime ago wrote for leave to appoint a Dep.ᵞ but should it not come in Time the Governor can on such an emergency grant 12 Months leave of absence and for that time appoint a Dep.ᵞ who I hope to get confirm'd in London in which event I shall be able to save more from the part I shall receive than from the whole Emoluments of my Office if I continue in this very expensive & to me disagreeable place, whenever I get my Affairs settled in London I propose to return either to the Highlands of Scotland or to the South of France as the Physicians shall direct till I can recover my Health and get clear of the heavy Burthen my long and very expensive attendance unavoidably brought me under, this I hope to

accomplish in about four years and then I flatter myself with the pleasing hope of passing the Even⁵ of my Life with some degree of independence & comfort in that dear Country called Old England which I must confess I would prefer to all others — I observe with the utmost Gratitude that you have Drawn only for the Principal of the Money you was generously Pleased to advance for me! I really want words to convey the Ideas of what I feel on this *Noble Act* and fresh mark of your uncommon Friendship, I pray Heaven may one day or other enable me to demonstrate by actions what words can so imperfectly express in the mean time accept my dear Friend of my most Gratefull Thanks —

The acco.ᵗˢ you indulge me with of some of the Officers of the Virginia Regiment are very pleasing, I often think of that Corps who ow'd it's distinguished Character to your Military Talents with uncommon satisfaction tho blended with much regret from the situation of many of its brave Officers, who certainly have not been rewarded in any degree ₐto their Merit ^{adequate} and uncommon Sufferings, I think without vanity we can assert that there never was and very probably never will be such another Provincial Regemᵗ I am truely glad that honest Weedon [1] (for whom I have a great regard) is well and still maintains the same happy flow of Spirits and Joyous turn for which he was always remark'd what is become of your Secretary Mᵣ Kirkpatrick whose lively Conversation and very Elegant Letters have so often made

---

[1] General George Weedon, of the Continental Army.

me happy? I see Mercer is appointed L<u>t</u> Gov<u>r</u> of N<u>o</u> Carolina but I do not yet learn whether it's intended as a real advantage or a mere Feather — I observe with great pleasure that you prosecute your great and arduous undertaking on the Dismal Swamp, I most sincerely wish that your most sanguine hopes may be fully gratified which would produce the most desirable end of encreasing that Fortune which you so highly deserve & at the same time shew the Colonists what enterprise & perseverance can effect — The discontents and heartburnings which were some time ago rekindled in the Continental Colonies and were once likely to be productive of very serious consequences gave me great uneasiness, But as that Subject has been so much and so often handled by the most masterly pens it would be extreme presumption in me to say anything upon it, especially to so excellent a Judge who is so immediatly interested as you are, I hope and very earnestly wish that Parliament may hit upon some expedient that will put all right again.

I am astonish'd how my Letters to you from London could have miscarried I generally ${}_\wedge$ Jack (your
^{sent} (inserted above) old Courier) who still lives with me to the Virginia Coffee House with them, for I very seldom went into the City which I hate, and Mercer can tell you how often I lamented the great misfortune of not hearing from you, tho' by incessant enquires I frequently had the great pleasure to hear of you. To recapitulate the various Planns I form'd to continue a Soldier and the infinite pains I took at different times to get into the Service of the East India Comp<u>y</u>, of Portugal

and at length of even Russia, the numberless incidents that concurr'd at different Periods to thwart my views and to destroy sometimes the fairest Prospects would fill a large Vol: that even to you who is pleased to interest yourself in so Friendly a manner would prove insupportably tedious and insipid, however as ᵧshew an inclination to be inform'd how I was disappointed in my Expedition to the Island of S.ᵗ John Please know that after reiterated applications, after the strongest assurances of Success, either a change of Ministers or Measures for in the course of our attendance there was no less than five different Lords presided at the Board of Trade constantly blasted our hopes for upwards of three years, in which time however the Island was Survey'd and laid off in Lots of Twenty thousand Acres each, a magnificent Plan of the whole on which each Lot was mark't & Num.ᵈ was sent by the Surveyor General to the above Board, and the Council at length determin'd that the Lots should be Drawn for by the different Memorialists at the Board of Trade & in presence of the Lords of that Board by way of Lottery, however they added so great a number to the original Claim.ᵗˢ, that very few got more than half a Lot and some not $^1/_{10}$.ᵗʰ — Cap.ᵗ Allanby late of the Navy a Gentleman of considerable Landed Property in the N. of England [1] and I had the good Fortune to Draw one of the best Lots between us, lying on the principal Harbour, he, his Lady and Family goes over there next Spring, but I dread that my inability of set-

---

[1] I find no mention of Captain Allanby in Burke's *Landed Gentry.*

tling my ten thousand Acres, and pressing demands to pay off old Scores will force me to Sell it for a trifle, the great number that were by Ministerial Interest admitted without any just claim disgusted several of Rank & Fortune for whom I was to have acted and made them relinquish their pretensions — I am one of those Officers who have commenced a Suit against the Great Rhansler of New York for a considerable part of his Estate in that Province,[1] where I understand it is given against us,

---

[1] NEW YORK 11th October 1764.

MY LORDS

Captain John Campbell late of his Majesty's 42d Regiment and several other Reduced officers of his Majesty's army, have presented Petitions to me, in consequence of the Royal Proclamation of the 7th of October 1763, Praying a Grant of Lands which lye within the pretended Bounds of a large Tract of Land claimed by one Renslaer. When the Petitions were laid before his Majestys Council, they were of opinion that it did not appear with sufficient clearness that the Lands were vacant, for them to advise me to grant them to the Petitioners. The officers resolved to abide in the suit they had commenced, & to carry their application to his Majesty, and at their desire, I inform your Lordships that I have seen the state of the Case which they have got drawn up by Mr Kemp, the Kings Attorney General for this Province, which may be depended on.

I imagine One single Observation will set the dispute in a clear Light before your Lordships.

Ranslaers Indian Purchase & Pattent extends from Hudsons River to a place call'd Wawaniaquasick which is therein said to be 24 miles from the River, Wawanioquasick is a heap of stones erected by the [Indians] as a Monument of some Memorable Event, & has been known by the Christians from the date of Mr Ranslaers Purchase down to the present time but is only nine Miles & three quarters from Hudsons River. It cannot be supposed that the Indians at that early Day, had any notion of English Miles, and even the Christians in computing distances thro' Woods, obstructed by Morasses Hills & Rivers have often supposed the distance double of what it was found to be when measured.

The Place & distance mention'd cannot both stand in construing the bounds given to this Tract; the Place is most certain, & by leaving out the Distance mentioned (24 Miles) and keeping to Wawaniaquasick, the Tract is clearly & distinctly bounded on all sides; whereas if we go beyond Wawaniaquasick, to the end of 24 Miles, no bounds are given for one very extensive side of the Tract, and that which Renslaer assumes gives him 170,000 acres. I am, my Lords, &c. (Governor Colder to the Board of Trade and Plantations.)

Although the governor of New York appears to have favored the suit of the officers, it was decided against them, and the estate remained intact in the possession of the Van Rensselaer family. Schuyler, in his *Colonial New York*, describes the entire tract as

which indeed we expected, but make no doubt of its being given in our favour by the King & Council, I was very active in this affair (in the course of which three Changes happen'd in Administration) however we with infinite pains got it passed the Board of Trade and afterwards the Council and at length got the Lords of the Treasury to agree that the Suit should be carried on at the Expence of the Crown a point of vast importance to half Pay Officers who had to Cope with a Man of vast Estate, which he and his Fore Fathers have long possess'd, We likewise obtain'd a Royal Instruction to the Gov.r & Attorney Gen.l of new York to prosecute the Suit with vigour & in the event of its being given against us to appeal forthwith, But procurings the Surveys, Copies of all the different Grants, Vouchers &c.a likewise defraying the Expences of the Officers employ'd in that Service and an infinite detail of Contingences cost a great deal of Money each pays according to his Rank I pay as L.t Col.o and consequently in case of Success will receive five thousand Acres, My Rank tho' well known to be in your Regem.t (I carefully avoided calling it a Provincial Corps) was never in the least objected to, either by any of those Great Boards nor by any of the Officers adventurers in this uncommon undertaking, the Lands are situated on the Banks of the River Hudson between the Cities of N York & Albany, and a great part of them highly cultivated—I have been often told in London that I was

being "twenty-four miles north and south, and forty-eight miles east and west," and that "it contained seven hundred thousand acres," adding that "the present cities of Albany and Troy are within its limits."

Virginia mad, I fear you will begin to think that I am become Land mad, but even should we miscarry which is exceedingly improbable I will in a few years get over it, and in case of Success I shall soon be reliev'd from my present Difficulties —

Your old Acquaintance Doc.ʳ Cockburn has been Dead some time, his widow is in the Country but I on rec.ᵗ of yours immediately waited on his Son and had the pleasure of delivering yours and your Lady's Message he herewith sends you a Letter —

Here we have nothing new or entertaining and as we have our News from the same Source with you it is almost impossible we can ever transmit you any. should no opport.ʸ offer soon from your River for this Island I beg you will do me the honor to write to me at London under cover to Lauchlin Macleane Esq.ʳ Queen Anne Street, Cavendish Square, Macleane is now become a Member of the British Senate and can in a very great degree enable us to carry on an uninterrupted Correspondence whatever part of Europe I may be in, than which nothing can be more agreeable to me —

I beg you will do me the honor to present my humble Respects to M.ʳˢ Washington in the warmest strain of affectionate Gratitude where are her Children? if in England I beg to know what place? that I may have the pleasure of waiting on them and paying them every degree of Respect and attention in my power — I ought now My dear Col.º to apologize for the tiresome length, inaccuracy and want of arrangement in the above Scrawl all I have to say is, that I cannot write you a short Letter tho' hur-

it, & shall then write you more fully, or endeavour to see you: in the mean Time pray commit to Writing such Hints as may occur.

Our All is at Stake, & the little Conveniencys & Comforts of Life, when set in Competition with our Liberty, ought to be rejected not with Reluctance but with Pleasure: Yet it is plain that in the Tob? Colonys We can't at present confine our Importations within such narrow Bounds as the Northern Colonys; a plan of this kind, to be practicable, must be adapted to our Circumstances; for not steadily executed, it had better have remained unattempted — We may retrench all Manner of Superfluitys, Finery of all Denominations, & confine ourselves to Linnens Woolens &c, not exceeding a certain price: it is amazing how much this (if adopted in all the Colonys) would lessen the American Imports, and distress the various Traders & Manufacturers in Great Britain — This wou'd quickly awaken their Attention — they woud see, they wou'd ^feel the Oppressions We groan under, & exert themselves to procure Us Redress: this once obtain'd, We shou'd no longer discontinue our Importations, confining ourselves still never to import any Article that shou'd hereafter be taxed by Act of Parliament for raising a Revenue in America; for however singular I may be in my Opinion, I am thoroughly convinced that (Justice & Harmony happily restored) it is not the Interest of these Colonies to refuse British Manufactures: our supplying our Mother-Country with gross Materials, & taking her Manufactures in Return is the true Chain of

Connection between Us ; these are the Bands, which, if not broken by Oppression, must long hold Us together, by maintain[in]g a constant Reciprocation of Interest: proper Caution shou'd therefore be used in drawing up the proposed plan of Association.   It may not be amiss to let the Ministry understand that until We obtain a Redress of Grievances, We will withhold from them our Commoditys, particularly refrain from making Tobacco, by which the Revenue would lose fifty times more than all their Oppressions cou'd raise here. —

Had the Hint I have given with regard to the Taxation of Goods imported into America been thought_{of} by our Merchants before the Repeal of the Stamp Act, the late American Revenue Acts wou'd probably never have been attempted. —

I am w.ᵗʰ Mᵣˢ Mason's Compˢ & my own to Yourself & Family

Dᵣ Sir

Yᵣ most obdᵗ Servᵗ

G MASON

PS —

Next Friday is the Day appointed
for the Meeting of the Vestry [1] ——

---

[1] " The Virginia vestry held a very unique place in the local system, for, besides electing churchwardens, presenting ministers to the governor for induction, providing glebes, 'parson houses,' and salaries, the vestry had, together with the churchwardens, charge of the poor, the processioning of the parish bounds, counting tobacco, and many minor duties." — CHANNING, in *Johns Hopkins University Studies.*

FROM GEORGE MASON, ESQ.

D^R S_{IR} GUNSTON HALL 23.rd April 1769.

Upon looking over the Association, of which I sent you a Copy, I have made some few Alterations in it, as ℔ Mem^{dm} on the other Side. —

I beg your Care of the inclosed Letters; & heartily wishing you (what I fear you will not have) an agreeable Session, I am D^r S^r

Y.^r most obed.^t Ser.^t

G MASON

PS

I shall take it as a particular
Favour if you'll be kind
enough to get me two
p.^r Gold snaps made at
W^{ms}burg for my little Girls;
they are small rings with a
joint in them, to wear in the
Ears, instead of Earrings: also
a p.^r of Toupee Tongs. —

Among the enumerated ~~Articles~~ Goods after the Articles Oyl & Fruit is added — Sugars — after Millenary of all Sorts is added — *Lace of all Sorts* — after the Article of Gauze is added (*except Boulting Cloaths*) —

In the fifth Resolve the Word — *Slaves* — in the second Line is struck out, & the word — *hereafter* — is added between the Word, any, & the Word, imported, — At the End of the Sixth Resolve after Tobacco-Debts, are added the Words — *due to them*

NB. the Reason of making this last Alteration is that at a time when the Government endeavours to call everything Seditious, it might be urged that the Subscribers took upon them a Sort of legislative Authority, in declaring they wou'd make Regulations relative to Tob? Debts, now they have an undoubted Right to make what Regulations they please in Debts due to themselves as the Option will still remain in the Debtors

Old Papers Respecting the Non-importation
of British Goods

1767
&
1774[1]

The Merchants, Traders, Gentlemen, and other principal Inhabitants of the Colony of Virginia in general & of the County of   in particular, deeply affected with the Grievances and Distresses with which his Majesty's American Subjects are oppressed, and dreading the evils which threaten the Ruin of themselves and their posterity, by reducing them from a free and happy people to a Wretched & miserable State of Slavery, having taken into their Serious Consideration the present State of the Trade of this Colony, and of the American Commerce in general, observe with anxiety that the Debt due to Great Britain for Goods imported from thence is very great, and the means of paying this Debt in the present Situation of affairs likely to become more and more precarious — that the Difficulties under which they now labour as a Trading people are owing to the Restrictions prohibitions, & ill advised Regulations in several late Acts of parliament in Great Britain; in particular that the last unconstitutional Acts imposing Duties on Tea, Paper, Glass &c.

---

1 This is Washington's indorsement, written on a small slip attached to these papers.

Provided always that the Goods shall not be delivered to the Person to whom they belong or to whom they are sent, untill advice is received that the late Revenue Acts against America are Repealed.

The following Agreement was entered into by the Merchants of Philadelphia the 10ᵗʰ March 1769.

The Merchants and Traders of the City of Philadelphia having taken into their serious consideration the present State of the Trade of this Province and of the American Commerce in general observe with Anxiety That the Debt due to Great Britain for Goods imported from thence is very great and the means of paying this Debt in the present situation of Affairs likely to become more and more precarious. That the difficulties under which they now labour as a Trading People are owing to the Restrictions, Prohibitions and ill advised Regulations in several late Acts of the Parliament of Great Britain in particular that the last unconstitutional Acts imposing Duties on Tea, Paper, Glass &c for the Sole purpose of raising a Revenue being injurious to Property and destructive to Liberty have a necessary Tendency to prevent the payment of old Debts or the contracting of New; & are of consequence ruinous to Trade. That notwithstanding the many earnest Applications already made there is little reason to expect a Redress of these Grievances. Therefore in Justice to themselves and their Posterity as well as to the Traders of Great Britain concerned in the American Commerce they have Voluntarily and Unanimously entered into the following Resolutions in hopes that their Example will Stimulate the Good People of this Province to be frugal in the Use & Consumption of British Manufacture and that their Brethren the Merchants and Manufacturers of Great Britain may from Motives of Friendship and Interest be engaged to exert themselves to obtain Redress of those Grievances under which the Trade and Inhabitants of America at present labour.

First Confirming the Agreement entered into the sixth of February last it is unanimously Resolved and Agreed. That the Subscribers will neither directly nor indirectly import from Great Britain nor any other part of Europe (except Linens & Provisions

from Ireland immediately) any kind of Goods Ship'd after the first of April next except the following Articles, Tin Plates, Wire, Powder, Shot, Lead, Sail Cloth, Wool Combs, Wool & Tow Cards, Sheerman Sheers Drugs Medicines, Dye Stuff, Salt, Coal, Brimstone, School Books, Sugar Moulds, Chalk and Whiting untill the late Acts imposing Duties on Tea, Glass &c for the purpose of raising a Revenue are repealed.

Secondly   That in all Orders which any of the Subscribers may send to Great Britain after the ninth instant for other Articles than those above enumerated they shall and will direct their Correspondents not to Ship them untill the above Acts are repealed.

Thirdly   That if any Person, Strangers or others shall Contrary to the Tenor of this Agreement import any Goods the Subscribers will by all lawfull & prudent Measures discountinance such Persons and will not purchase any Goods so imported.

Fourthly   That these Resolves shall be binding on all and each of the Subscribers who do hereby each and every Person for himself upon his Word & Honour agree that he will Strictly and firmly adhere to and abide by every Article of this Agreement from this time for and during the Continuance of the above mentioned Acts or untill a General Meeting of the Subscribers after three Days Public Notice shall determine otherwise.

Annapolis March   1769

Gentlemen

We are favor'd with a Letter from you of the 15th Current directed to us, in behalf of the Merchants and Traders of this place inclosing a Copy of an Agreement entered into by the Merchants and Traders of your City respecting the non-importation of certain Goods from Great Britain untill the repeal of the several Acts of Parliament laying oppressive and unconstitutional taxes on the American Colonies.   Truly Sensible of the expediency of the measures recommended by you, we immediately on receipt of your Letter procured a meeting of all the Gentlemen concern'd in Trade in this City, and they having considered the Matter so far as the time and circumstances would allow, have desired us to communicate their sentiments to you on that Subject.

The Agreement entered into by you is approved of by the Merchants here and they have Unanimously resolved to pursue such a Plan, provided the importers of the Province in general or nearly so, can be brought into the like measure.

But the Importers of Goods in this City are so few in number when compared to those of the whole Province that it would be in vain for them to Attempt the puting such a Scheme in execution without a general Concurrance. To obtain which the Merchants here will exert themselves not only by shewing their readiness to enter into the proposed Measure, but by their communicating your Letter and forwarding therewith a Copy of your Agreement to the Principal Merchants throughout the Province. Which step at their last meeting they desired us to pursue with all convenient speed and is now in great forwardness.

You must no doubt be sensible from your knowledge of the different manner in which the Trade of this Province and Pensilvania is carried on, that such an Agreement as yours cannot be so readily entered into here as in your Province. The Importers in the one are chiefly if not wholly confined to the City of Philadelphia; but in Maryland the Merchants are Scattered all over the Province consequently their general Consent to any particular measure cannot be readily Obtained. However that Difficulty might be easily got over if the Importation of Goods was entirely confind to Merchants; But here every Gentleman and Planter Imports Goods more or less for their Family use by which means [I] may venture to say that not above   of the Goods brought into this Province are imported by the Merchants & Traders. Such being the case not only the Consent of the Merchant importers is necessary, but that of all the Gentlemen & Planters who import Goods for their own use, otherwise the end proposed by the Agreement would be entirely defeated.

We must likewise observe that when the Agreement for not importing Goods is entered into here, many Articles must be added to those exceptions in yours which the circumstance of the Province will render absolutely necessary tho' they may not be so in Pensilvania.

But we shall Write you more fully on this Subject when we receive Answers to the several Letters which we have sent out, and in the mean time have only to Assure you that we have no

reason to doubt, but that the Scheme will ˄meet universal Approbation. We are

Gentⁿ

Your mo : Obᵗ Hble Servants

JAMES DICK & STEWART

NICHˢ MACCUBBIN

CHARLES WALLACE

WILLIAM STEWART

ANNAPOLIS March 25ᵗʰ 1769

GENTLEMEN

Last Monday we received a letter from the merchants in Philadelphia, relative to an agreement they have entered into for the non importation of certain goods from Great Britain. ——

Having communicated the Same to the Merchants here they have directed us to transmit a Copy thereof to you together with a Copy of said agreement and a Copy of our letter in answer thereto. All which we Submit ˄to your Consideration and that of the other Merchants and Importers to whom it is Convenient for you to communicate the same. And we beg your Opinion thereon when you have duly considered the matter and We are

Respectfully Gentlemen ——

Your mo hble Servᵗˢ

JAMES DICK & STEWART

NICHˢ MACCUBBIN

CHARLES WALLACE

WILLIAM STEWART [1]

WILLIAMSBURG, May 31, 1774.[2]

GENTLEMEN,

Last *Sunday* Morning several Letters were received from *Boston, Philadelphia,* and *Maryland,* on the most interesting and

---

[1] These letters and papers from Pennsylvania and Maryland Washington inclosed to George Mason, April 5, 1769, with an accompanying letter commending the "scheme," and asking Mason's opinion as to how and when it would be best to promote it in Virginia.

[2] This is a *broadside,* and is one of the papers which Washington has fastened together and labeled "Old Papers Respecting Non-importation of British Goods."

important Subject of *American* Grievances. The Inhabitants of *Boston* seem to be in a most piteous and melancholy Situation, and are doubtful whether they will be able to sustain the impending Blow without the Assistance and Cooperation of the other Colonies. By the Resolutions of their Town Meeting, it appears to be their Opinion that the most effectual Assistance which can be given them by their Sister Colonies will arise from a general Association against Exports and Imports, of every Kind, to or from *Great Britain*. Upon Receipt of this important Intelligence, the Moderator judged it most prudent immediately to convene as many of the late Representatives as could be got together,[1] and yesterday, at a Meeting of twenty five of the late Members, we took the Business under our most serious Consideration. Most Gentlemen present seemed to think it absolutely necessary for us to enlarge our late Association, and that we ought to adopt the Scheme of Nonimportation to a very large Extent; but we were divided in our Opinions as to stopping our Exports. We could not, however, being so small a Proportion of the late Associates, presume to make any Alteration in the Terms of the general Association, and therefore resolved to invite all the Members of the late House of Burgesses to a general Meeting in this City on the first Day of *August* next. We fixed this distant Day in Hopes of accommodating the Meeting to every Gentleman's private Affairs, and that they might, in the mean Time, have an Opportunity of collecting the Sense of their respective Counties. The Inhabitants of the City were convened yesterday in the Afternoon, and most chearfully acceded to the Measures we had adopted.

We flatter ourselves it is unnecessary to multiply words to induce your Compliance with this Invitation, upon an Occasion which is, confessedly, of the most lasting Importance to all *America*. Things seem to be hurrying to an alarming Crisis, and demand the speedy, united Councils of all those who have a Regard for the common Cause. We are, Gentlemen, your most affectionate Friends, and obedient humble Servants,

PEYTON RANDOLPH, Moderator; ROBERT C. NICHOLAS, EDMUND PENDLETON, WILLIAM HARWOOD, RICHARD ADAMS, THOMAS

[1] The Governor had dissolved the Assembly on May 27.

WHITING, HENRY LEE, LEMUEL RIDDICK, THOMAS JEFFERSON, MANN PAGE, JUNIOR, CHARLES CARTER, LANCASTER, JAMES MERCER, ROBERT WORMELEY CARTER, GEORGE WASHINGTON, FRANCIS LIGHTFOOT LEE, THOMAS NELSON, JUNIOR, ROBERT RUTHERFORD, JOHN WALKER, JAMES WOOD, WILLIAM LANGHORNE, THOMAS BLACKBURNE, EDMUND BERKELEY, JOHN DONELSON, PAUL CARRINGTON, LEWIS BURWELL.

FROM SAMUEL GIST, ESQ.

LONDON June 17ᵗʰ 1769 —

SIR

I take this opportunity to acquaint you of the Death of Mʳ ₍Capel₎ Hanbury & as he chiefly managed the Business it will Probably be a means of some of their Friends changeing their Corrospondants here, I therefore beg leave to Offer you my best Services & to assure you if it suits you to make Tryal of me that you shall be dealt with by the Strictest Rules of Justice & Honor —

There is very little Tobacco at present in this Market & what comes home this Year will sell well, I am very Respecᵗ

Sir Your most Obed Sᵗ

SAMˡ GIST

FROM THOMAS H. MARSHALL, ESQ.

MARYLAND the 18ᵗʰ of June 1769

SIR/

Having sum Company, and the Wind Blowing fresh, Prevented my Attending on you this day, as

Intended: However immagin this may satisfy you, in Answer to your's, by M.ʳ Lund Washington, Relative to my Lands in Virginia — I would Readily make an Exchange, for M.ʳ Alexander's Land on this side, Provided I could be made safe in Regard to Conveyance, As his Wife is not of sufficient Age to Co[n]vey the same, And the Land Under a Strong Intale, However that would be Easilly wiped of, (heare) was M.ʳˢ Alexander of Suffitiant age — On your giveing me a suffitiant Indemnification in Regard to M.ʳ Alexanders Land bein made over to me &c. when his Wife is Qualified so to do, And we can Agree on the Part of the Land you will Take in Exchange, Shall be Ready to Comply. And as to the Ballance of my Land in Virginia, (When An oppertunity shall offer, that I can make a Conveneant Purchase heare) Will Let you have the Remainder at 40/ Virginia Cur.ʸ P.ʳ Acc.ᵗ, Paid in English Gun.ˢ Pistoles & Silver Dol.ˢ or Ither of them, at their Current Value, — these Are the Terms, and no Other that will Induce me to Part with my Virginia Land, And as I am not well Acquainted with the Situation thereof Should be Greatly oblige to you for the Platt you sent over to me sum time ago, by M.ʳ Lund Washington which will Take Care of and Return safe

I am S.ʳ your Most Hble Serv.ᵗ

THO.ˢ HA.ᴺ MARSHALL

FROM EDMUND PENDLETON, ESQ.[1]

D.R SIR

I have at last found leisure to peruse & consider the papers you left with me for my Opinion on the nature of your Interest in your Fairfax Lands.[2]

The deed of Settlement made by your Father on your brother Lawrence is long & complicated occasioned chiefly by an Intention to provide against the contingencie of the Prince W.m Lands which were the Subject of that deed & the Wesmoreland Lands Formerly Settled upon Augustine, from coming into the same hands by the death of one of your brothers without Issue, but as I take it for granted that your brother Aug.t chose to keep the Westmorl.d Lands, & not to give them up & take to the Prince William Lands as he had Power to do upon the death of Lawrence without Issue, great part of that settlement is of little consequence, as to the Point you Now want to be Satisfied in.

The Prince William Lands then are limited to Lawrence in fee simple upon the Contingencie of his *leaving Issue at his death :* He takes notice of a daughter in his will & if she survived him, your fathers Will has no operation upon the estate, but it must go according to the Will of y.r brother Lawrence by which you take an estate tail, with a remainder to your brother Aug.t in fee simple. For tho' the words of the devising clause would give you

---

[1] Born in Caroline County, Virginia, September 9, 1721; died in Richmond, October 23, 1803. Philip Pendleton, grandfather of Hon. Edmund Pendleton, came to this country in 1676.

[2] For wills of Lawrence and Augustine Washington, see Appendix.

a fee, yet by a Subsequent one he directs that if you, Sam!, John & Charles or any of you, die *without Lawful Issue* such Land as was given you or any of you, would become the property of ~~you or any of you~~ his brother Augustine & his heirs forever, which changes your & their Estates in all the Lands Claimed under his Will into estates tail.

If indeed the daughter of Lawrence died before him, then as he left no Issue, The Land by the Settlement was to be subject to your father's disposition and by his Will, you have a fee simple in the Prince William Lands, under the Remainder limited to you if Law. died without Issue, since one of the contingencies upon wch you were to have a fee, has happened, that of your arriving to full age, altho' you have no Issue. If this latter was the case, and you would choose to support y^r fee simple, it might be proper to bring a Bill in Chancery to Perpetuate testimony to prove the fact of her dying before her father, as without testimony the presumption would be that she survived, being named in his Will; Nothing Further Occurs to me necessary to be mentioned. I am

Sir

Your mo: Ob! ħble Serv!

Edm^D Pendleton

July 3^d 1769.

———

FROM THE REVEREND JONATHAN BOUCHER.

Sir

In Consequence of your L^r, Mast^r Custis now waits on You; & as this is a pretty busy Time with Us in

School, I shall be glad He may set off back again at y.ᵉ same Time You do for the Springs.

Enclosed You have his Acc.ᵗ for y.ᵉ last Year, which as You were so obliging as to offer Me when I was at Mount Vernon, I will beg y.ᵉ Fav.ʳ of You now to send by Jack. I hope it will not appear too high ᵗᵒ You ; it being just what I charged y.ᵉ only Boy (M.ʳ Turner) I ever had living w.ᵗʰ Me in y.ᵉ same Manner He does. For my own Part, I must own to You, I charge his Horses merely by Guess, hav.ᵍ never very nearly attended to y.ᵉ Expence of maintain.ᵍ a Horse : Those I have mentioned y.ᵉ Matter to here, think it too low : You, probably, may have had Occasion to consider y.ᵉ Matter, & therefore I beg Leave to refer it entirely to y.ʳself. I have yet to mention to You on this Subj.ᵗ, that, persuaded by my own Experience, I have lately come to a Resolu.ⁿ of tak.ᵍ no more Boys for less than £25 ℔.ʳ Ann : There are now four upon these Terms, & more expected soon. Unless therefore You object to it in Time, You must expect next Year to find your Son charged so too.

I have a Pleasure in informing You that I please Myself w.ᵗʰ thinking We now do much better than formerly : You will rem.ʳ my hav.ᵍ complain'd of Jack's Laziness, which, however, I now hope is not incurable. For I find He will bear driving, which heretofore I us'd to fear He would not. He has met w.ᵗʰ more Rig.ʳ since I saw You than in all y.ᵉ Time before, & He is the better for it. This I mean only as to his Books ; in other Matters He is faultless. His new Boy too is infinitely fitter, for him than Julius ; & if He be not spoil'd here, which, in Truth,

credible damage below; all the Fother entirely lost and the Corn blown down, Tob.º that was in the Fields lost and several Ships &c drove ashoar, we have suffer'd in this Neighbourhood yet not considerably. Our Election comes on next Monday, cannot say who will be our Burgesses [1] tho' expect B. Grymes will be one altho' every Man of any tolerable understanding I believe will be against him. M.ʳ Dixon & M.ʳ Marye [2] are the other two that offer and it's believ'd M.ʳ Dixon will be chosen I am

D.ʳ Sir your most Affec.ᵗ Hum.ᵉ Serv.ᵗ

FIELDING LEWIS

FROM MR. MOSES MONTGOMERIE.

SIR

Nothing else than M.ʳ Grayson's not returning Home untill the day before yesterday, could have prevented me from giving you an answer relative to the payment of M.ʳˢ Savages annuity long before this time — I now beg leave to inform you, that it is his opinion as well as myne, that it would not be prudent or safe in me to answer your demand in behalf of M.ʳˢ Savage. With my best respects to M.ʳˢ Washington

I remain Sir
Your most ob.ᵗ Serv.ᵗ

MO.ˢ MONTGOMERIE

5.ᵗʰ October 1769

---

[1] According to Washington's copy of the *Virginia Almanac* for 1769 the Representatives from Spotsylvania were Benjamin Grymes and Fielding Lewis, and for 1770 Benjamin Grymes and Roger Dixon.

[2] Peter Marye.

FROM CAPTAIN WILLIAM CRAWFORD.

SIR

They Survayʳˢ is to be [here] to survay your Land soon and will want there cash which I have not for them

You may send it by Mʳ Harrison sealᵈ up in a Letter to me half Joes or Pensilvania mony will sute best for them

I beleve no Person interfares with you — I shall have the [w]hole Run out before the Surwayʳ comes on the spot   I have bin unwell or I would have had it don befor now I shall have that Land Entred¹ and survayᵈ and shall joyn another survay to it if I can that you had of my Brother as Mʳ Harrison will be up befor I shall have it don you give me your sentiments on it.   I beleve I can make about 700 Acres there or may be more As to news I shall Referr you to Mʳ Harrison

I am Sir Your most Humᵉ Sarvat

W CRAWFORD

OLD TOWN Octʳ 13ᵗʰ 1769

═══════

FROM MR. ROBERT ALEXANDER.²

SIR/

I have examined the Books and find a Ballance of about two hundred pounds Curʸ due from us to Mʳ

---

¹ The Pennsylvania Land Office was, on the 3d of April, 1769, opened for the location of lands in that province, west of the Alleghany Mountains, below Kittanning. — BUTTERFIELD.

² The ancestor of the Alexander family in Virginia was John Alexander, who settled in Northampton County in 1659.

Fielding Lewis on Acc.! of his Wife's Fortune, which please to pay to M.! Lewis, or otherwise, dispose of it (according to his order) in the purchase of Negroes — or any other manner, as you shall think most proper, and the first time I see you will give you a receipt for the said Sum in the interim I am y.! humble S.!

ROB.! ALEXANDER

Octob.! 27.!! 1769 —

FROM CAPTAIN DANIEL M.ᶜCARTY.[1]

Dec.! 6.!! 1769 —

SIR

I send you by M.! Pierce Bayly the Deeds made by me, and my wife to M.! Chichester, and likewise them from him, and his wife, to me, as also my Grandfathers will, Wherein you will find in the 3.ᵈ Page how he Gave the Land, Fairfax County was then Stafford, and by Looking over the will you may see some hardships which my father was laid Under more than Either of his Brothers — My wifes fathers will I have not, neither is it in my Power to Get it at this time, it being on the Records of Lancaster but you may see by the Deeds made to M.! Chichester in what it was Given, Which I hope will be Sufficient — We have at last had a Vestry to lay the Parish Levy which is Sixty three ℔ Pole 34900 being Levy'd Towards Paying for the Church, and by those Very

---

1 Captain, afterwards Colonel, Daniel McCarty, of Pope's Creek, Westmoreland County, married Winifred, daughter of Francis and Sarah (Fitzhugh) Thornton, of "Society Hill."

Gentlemen who was so much against it formerly, Mrs Posey and old Mrs Johnston are both Dead within two or three Days of Each other — You will Remember that I informed you that I have Near Six thousand acres of Land more which is all intail'd lying in the County of Loudoun, and I must beg your Care of the Papers Now sent, My Wife Joyns me in our Compliments to your Self, Mrs Washington, and Miss Patsy, hopeing to see you all Return in Good health, And I Remain with Great Esteem

Dr Sr Y^r Most
Obe^t Hb^le Servt

N. B. I never Rec^d y^r   Daniel McCarty
Letter Untill the 24th of
Nov^r —

FROM THE REVEREND JOSIAH JOHNSON.[1]

Decr 20th 1769.

Sir /

It is with great Pleasure I ~~now~~ sit down to inform you, that it is now in my Power to contribute my little Mite of Service to one of the gallant Defenders of ~~his~~ their Country. Nor shou'd I (however cautious it may be necessary to be in general) have hesitated a Moment to have given my hearty Assent, when you first did me the Honor of applying to me on the Subject of appointing Mr Crawford Surveyor of ye 200,000 Acres[2] specified, had I not been apprehensive, that

---

[1] Rev. Josiah Johnson, master of grammar school, William and Mary, married Mildred Moody, May 26, 1768. He died in 1773, leaving no issue.

[2] The land on the Ohio granted by Virginia to the officers and soldiers of the Virginia regiment who served in the French and Indian War.

it might interfere with a prior Engagement I lay under to M.ʳ May. While this doubt subsisted, Col. Washington wou'd, I am confident, have condemned me, if I had entered upon a new Resolution; but it is now totally removed, & he may depend upon my Concurrence.

                    I am
                         S.ʳ/
            with great Respect
                .   Your very humble Servant
                              JOSIAH JOHNSON.

_____

FROM THE REVEREND JAMES HORROCKS.

SIR/

I am much obliged to you for the clear Account you have been pleased to send me to Day concerning the Lands to be surveyed.

I dare say you will agree with me in Opinion that it is for the Honor of the College as well as the interest of the Officers & Soldiers, that (to use the Words of the Council) " a Person properly qualified to survey these Lands be appointed by us — I have no Doubt of M.ʳ Crawford's being such as you have mention'd, & I beg Leave to assure you very sincerely that this my first Duty to the College being satisfied, I shall be happy in the Opportunity of shewing due Respect to the Advice of the Honb.ˡᵉ The Governor & Council, & of properly Regarding Col : Washington's Recommendation —

I have communicated to M.ʳ Johnson my Senti-

ments on this Subject, & I believe his agree very
much with mine — M.ͬ Camm [1] is not in Town & I
imagine we shall not be collected again till after the
Holy Days — I am of Opinion it wou'd be adviseable for M.ͬ Crawford to be here as soon as possible,
I mean with his own Convenience, as I see no Im-
pediment to retard or prevent his Success.

I can, Sir, say no more with Propriety, & therefore
I am sure you will not expect more than this —
　　　I have the Honor to be
　　　　　　　with great Respect
W.ᴹ & MARY　　　　　Your very Humble Ser.ᵗ
Dec.ͬ 21. 1769.　　　　　　　J. HORROCKS

FROM DE BERDTS, LEE, & SAYRE.

LONDON Jan: 27. 1770.

SIR,

Having determined to make an essay of the tob.º
trade we have bo't the Liberty a new ship, which
Cap.ᵗ Walker now carrys out to load for us in Potomac,
and as we design her to be a regular annual ship,
our friends will always have a certain conveyance for
their goods, & their tob.º to market. Being determin'd to act on an upright plan, we beg the favour
of your assistance to Cap.ᵗ Walker, & can assure you
that if we are so happy as to receive your tob.º no
House will be more assiduous for your interest either
in the sale of y.ͬ tob.º or in the purchase of your
goods. If it sh.ᵈ be at any time convenient for you
to lodge money in our hands, we shall very willingly

---

1 Rev. John Camm, president of William and Mary College from 1771 to 1777.

allow you the full benefit in discounting the dutys
on y.ʳ tob.º — Cap.ᵗ Walker will send to York river so
that he can easily take tob.ºˢ from thence & we hope
you will favor us with some of yours.

Our Comp.ᵗˢ to M.ʳˢ Washington & y.ʳ family & with
esteem remain

Sir, y.ʳ mo: ob.ᵗ h̶b̶l̶e̶ Serv.ᵗˢ

De Berdt's, Lee & Sayre
Dennys De Berdt
Dennis De Berdt Jun.ʳ
William Lee
Stephen Sayre

FROM THOMAS H. MARSHALL, ESQ.

March the 8ᵗʰ 1770

Sir/

On my way to my Quarter on this side (this day)
I observed several Valuable Trees &c. cut down
Worked and Working up, on my Land; as they are on
that Part the Land we was on Making An Exchange,
for the same Quantity in Maryland, Induces me to
Immagen, you miss apprehended me in my offer's to
you Relative to the same. Which I Remember well
was neare as Followes, when I was at your House, I
made this offer, that I would Exchange ^the Land I held
Between the Mane Rode and Potowmack River, for
the same Quantity of Land (off M.ʳ Alexanders) to
be laid off Sutable to my Plantation in Maryland,
Provided I could have the same in Immediate Use,
which was then agreed to, Provided M.ʳ Alexander

could so Dispose the same ; — At Poseys sale you
mentioned to me, you should be Glad to have that
Matter settled Before you Went down the Cuntry, as
you wanted (If the Exchange could be now made)
to order sum Rales &c. cutt off the Part of Land,
On which we Prevailed on M.ʳ Alexander to cross the
Riv.ʳ with me that Evening, in order to Look at the
Land, and the Part I would Exchange for, which he
did, tho' then did not chuse to give Any Determined
Answer, On my Seing you the Next Day (at the
Sale) I acquainted you Therewith, on which you
seemed still desirous of being on sum Sertenty before
you Left home, I then tould you I Immagened it
Would make Little Differance, for as soon as M.ʳ
Alexander should agree to the Part I was to Take of
his Land, I would then Acquant M.ʳ Lund Washing-
ton thereof when he might Proceed as you should
Instruct.   I never could get any Sertenty from M.ʳ
Alexander, Consequently could not give any such
Information.   Indeed on ˄the first of Jan.ʸ last I sent to
M.ʳ Alexander Pressing him to Let me be on sum
Sertenty (Inclosing him a Ruff Draft of the Plat of
his Land, Shewing the Part I would have [a line mutilated]
Any Particular Part of the Land, I would [mutilated]
Any Part for you, But think its out of my Power
this Year [mutilated] it Before &c.   The Reason M.ʳ
Alexander Mention's Peavock, (his [mutilated] I would
have had, took from his Plantation, tho', Let a Viny
[mutilated] for his fence, However on the Rec.ᵗ of M.ʳ
Alexanders [mutilated] myself no farther Trouble, Not

APPENDIX

WILL OF JOHN CUSTIS.[1]

In the Name of God Amen I John Custis Esqr. of Northampton County in Virginia being at present in perfect Health and sound in memory, thanks be to the Almighty, but considering the State of Mankind, how soon they are taken out of this life, and being willing to Settle those Worldly Goods, God of his infinite mercy and goodness far beyond my deserts, he hath bestowed upon me, do make, ordain, and appoint this my last Will and Testament revoking all former Wills and Deeds of Gift whatever.

Imprimis I Give my Soul to God, that gave it me, my Body I Give to the Earth from whence it came, to have a decent Burial at the discretion of my executors hereafter named, no ways doubting through the Mercy and merits of my dear Saviour Christ Jesus to have a joyful resurrection.

Item my Will and desire is, that my dear and loving Wife Sarah Custis live during pleasure at my now dwelling House, and Plantation at Hungars not to be disturbed by any pretence whatever while she liveth, but if it please God she Marries, her Husband immediately enter into Bond with Security to keep all the Housing, fencing, and Plantation in good repair, and in Case of failure my son Hancock Custis, or his heirs enter into the said Houses, and Plantation the Bond to be made to Hancock Custis, or his heirs, in the sum of five hundred Pounds Sterling.

Item My Will and desire is, that my dear Wife Sarah Custis have, besides what I shall hereafter give her the feather Bed & Furniture, we usely lye on, one pair of good Sheets, one pair of Blankets, her choice of all my riding Horses with her riding furniture with her choice of any Copper Kettle she please.

---

1 Son of the Honorable John Custis, of Arlington, born 1652, died January 26, 1713. He married first Margaret, daughter of Mr. John Michaell, second Sarah, daughter of Colonel Southey Littleton.

ITEM I Give and bequeath unto my said dear Wife all the Negros & Slaves of what sort soever, that I had with her, I likewise give her my Mulattoe Woman Chocolate withall her increase that she now hath or shall have, my Negro men named Peter, and Trout, and my girl Dennis to her, and her heirs forever.

ITEM I lend to my said Wife during her Widowhood, my Negro man called Michael, my Indian Woman called Sarah, and my Mulattoe Girl called Emananuel. But in case of my said Wifes Death or marriage, then the said Slaves to return to those that I shall hereafter give them to, in this Will, and my Negro man Bristol during her Widowhood, this with my hand.

ITEM My Will and desire is, that what goods, Household Stuff, Cattle, and Sheep, I have hereafter given to my Children, the like proportionable part shall be set apart for my now Wife before the rest of my Estate be divided, the particulars of which, I shall hereafter insert.

ITEM I give and bequeath to my son John Custis [1] my Chiconessex Plantation with all the Stock that shall be found thereon of what nature soever to him and his heirs forever. I likewise give to my said son Arlington House together with two hundred and fifty Acres of Land thereto belonging which I bought of Mr William Willett, and have Patent for it, in my own name with the Appurtenances thereto belonging to him and his heirs forever.

ITEM I Give and bequeath unto my said son all my Stock of Male Cattle, that be found upon Smiths Island, and Mackean Island after my decease, I say Male Cattle with my own hand.

ITEM I likewise give and bequeath unto my said Son one large Silver Dish, six large Silver Plates, one large Silver Bason, two Silver Candlesticks, with a Silver Snuff Dish, and two Silver Snuffers, one good feather Bed, and furniture, and the second choice of my riding Horses, my best Saddle and furniture, and his choice of my Cases of Pistols, and Holsters, and my best Sword to him and his heirs forever.

ITEM I Give and bequeath unto my son Hancock Custis after my dear Wifes decease or relinquishment, my now dwelling House & Plantation containing fifteen hundred Acres of Land withall the Appurtenances thereunto belonging during his natural life to-

---

[1] Father of Daniel Parke Custis.

gether with that Tract of Land, I bought of Captain Isaac Fox-
craft containing by estimation three hundred and forty Acres of
Land (be the same, more or less) commonly called and known by
the Davis, with that Land I bought of Pierce Davis, which makes
upon that quantity, and after his decease, to the heir of his Body
lawfully begotten (That is to say) it is my true intent and meaning, that my said son hath power to divide the said Land between
two of his issue Male_∧and what quantity he shall think fit, and
they to enjoy it, and their heirs forever. But if it should happen that my said son should dye, without heir Male, then I Give
it to his heirs female, and their heirs forever, but for want of
such heir to my heir at common Law forever.

ITEM   I Give and bequeath unto my said son Hancock Custis,
and his heirs forever, my Plantation at Jolys Neck in Accomack
County containing by estimation two thousand Acres of Land
together with three hundred Acres of Swamp low Land lying near
the Land, I sold to William Bradwater, which I have reserved
for Timber for the supply of the two thousand Acres of Land
which I Give to my said son, and his heirs forever. But it is my
Will & desire that my now Wife Sarah Custis have free liberty
of range of twenty Steers during her natural life, all the rest of
my Land lying at Pocomock that I shall_∧be disposed of ; in my
lifetime, I Give and bequeath to my son John Custis, and his heirs
and assigns forever.

ITEM   I Give and bequeath unto my son Hancock Custis besides
what already I have given him, these following Negros & Slaves
(Viz) Simon, Dum, Harry, Bristol, Michael and Emmanuel always
excepted, that my Wife have the use of the said Michael and
Emmanuel as before excepted in my Will : — and Bristol.

ITEM   I Give and bequeath unto my son Henry Custis five hundred, & fifty Acres of Land on Jingoteague Island which I had
of Captain William Kendall together with an Island adjoining
thereto by a Bridge commonly called and known by the name of
wild Cat Island by estimation two hundred and fifty acres of
Land withall Marshes and other advantages thereto belonging to
him the said Henry Custis, and his heirs and assigns forever ;
Always Provided, and it is my Will and desire that my now Wife
have liberty of range for twenty Steers upon the said Island dur-

ing her natural life, with free liberty of bringing of and carrying _∧ at her pleasure.
^{on}

ITEM I Give and bequeath unto my said Son Henry Custis
these following Negros and Slaves (Viz.) Daniel at Pocomock,
Ben, Bull, Jack, Rufby, the boy Will, Bridget, and Lankeston to
him the said Henry Custis his heirs and assigns forever.

ITEM I Give and bequeath unto my two daughters Elizabeth Custis
and Sorrowful Margaret Kendall five hundred Acres of Land _∧ I
^{which}
bought of Henry Towles lying and being on Jingoteague Island
in Accomack County together with an Island that I bought of
Joh— Morris in the said County containing by estimation three
hundred Acres of Land, and Marsh, to be held in common between the two Sisters during their natural lives, and after their
decease to any two Children of their Bodies lawfully begotten,
And if it should happen that either of my two daughters should
dye without issue, then her part to be and remain to the issue living of either of their Bodies, and their Heirs forever, and in case
of failure of any such Heir, then I Give and bequeath the said
Land to my Son Henry Custis his heir and Assigns forever, the
true intent and meaning of this my Will is, if the issue of either
or both of my said Daughters enter upon the Premises at full age,
then they or either of them enjoy the said Land, and their heir
forever, my meaning is that my daughters, or their now Husbands
give the Land above given to which Child they please of my
daughters body begotten.

ITEM I Give unto my said daughter Elizabeth Custis these following Negro Slaves (to wit) George, Sunto, Daniel, her Son Lucretia,
her daughter Yamnone Indian Sarah, and her son Jemme, and
Notse to her during her natural life, and for the life of her Husband
Thomas Custis, and after their decease them and their increase I
Give to any Child or Children of their Body lawfully begotten, but
for want of any such Issue, then to Thomas Custis her husband,
and his heirs forever. Always provided that my now Wife hath
the use of the Indian Woman Sarah during her Widowhood.

ITEM I Give and bequeath unto my daughter Sorrowful Margaret
Kendall these following Negros or Slaves Nicholas, Jenny his
Wife Abigail, Moriah, John a boy, all children of the said Jenny,

Indian Betty, Lettitia, Festus, withall their increase, that they ever shall have, my Negro man named Cesar to her my said daughter during her natural life, and for the life of her Husband William Kendall, and after their decease to be to the issue of the said Sorrowful Margaret Kendall of her body lawfully begotten to one or more, as he shall think fit, and for want of such Issue, then to the said William Kendall and his heirs forever.

ITEM I Give to my boy John Atkinson a Horse, four Cows, and Calfs, four Ewes, and Lambs, one feather Bed, bolster, one pair of Sheets, two Blankets, and one Rug, and if it should happen that I should dye having either Sloop, or Sloops the said John Adkinson to take his choice of them, with their Apparrel, all which I Give to the said John Atkinson his heirs and assigns forever, but my will is, that the said John Adkinson live with my now Wife until he is at the age of one and twenty, unless my now Wife cause to the contrary in whose hands I leave every particular given to be delivered at the aforesaid age, or sooner if she think fit.

ITEM I Give and bequeath unto Sarah Custis Matthews two Cows and two Ewes.

ITEM I Give and bequeath unto Yardly Michael the remaining part of that Tract of Land, I bought of Joseph Benthall Sen[r] him and his heirs forever, Always provided that [whoever?] lives upon my Plantation at Hungars have liberty to get Timber thereon for the use of this Plantation, I now live on.

ITEM I give and bequeath unto my daughter Elizabeth Custis my Negro man Toney besides what I have already given her, to her and her heirs forever. Upon mature and deliberate consideration relating to all the Negros and Slaves given to my aforesaid two daughters Elizabeth Custis and Sorrowful Margaret Kendall, and the more fuller to explain my meaning and *will* I do make void the word give, and I do lend the said Negros and Slaves during the lives of my said two daughters, and their husbands, and in Case it should happen that either of my said two daughters dye Childless, they shall have liberty to dispose of the said Negros and Slaves to any of their relations as they shall think most fit.[1]

---

[1] It is interesting to note that John Custis in disposing of his slaves seems to have desired to prevent the breaking up of families among them.

ITEM I Give and bequeath unto my Son John Custis, my quarter part of the Brigenteen the Northampton ; built by John Bowdoin, and to his Assigns forever and I likewise give to my said Son John Custis, my bigest Silver Tankard, and likewise my father's picture now standing in my Hall.

ITEM I Give to my Wife Sarah Custis, my next largest Silver Tankard.

ITEM I Give and bequeath unto Elias Taylor of Accomack County five hundred Acres of Land lying and being at Acaconson in the said County to him and his heirs forever. Always provided, and it is my true intent and meaning that the said Taylor pay to my executors hereafter named, the sum of seventy pounds Sterling by good acceptable Bills of exchange, and fifteen thousand pounds of good Tobacco and Cask according to a Verbal agreement made between us which if he refuseth then I do empower my executors hereafter named to make Sale of the said Land for the best advantage they can.

ITEM I Give and bequeath unto Henry Toles of Accomack County and to his heirs and assigns forever five hundred Acres of Land lying and being at Pocomock near Hyleys Neck according to an Agreement made between us, and likewise ten thousand Nails, Always provided that he makes over, all his right, title and Interest of five hundred Acres of Land which he lives on : on Jingoteague Island, and acknowledge the same in Accomack County Court to those Persons, that I [have] given it to, by Will, and in the same nature.

ITEM My Will is that before — my Estate is divided, these goods hereafter excepted, or the worth of them, be set apart for use of my now Wife, it being to make her part even of what I have given before to my Children, three feather Beds, Bolsters & Pillows, three Rugs, three Blankets, two sutes of Curtains and Vallens, ten pair of Sheets, eight pair of pillowbeers, eight Towels, five dozen of Napkins, six Table Cloths, ten pewter dishes, two Basons, three dozen of Plates, one Chamber Pot, two Candlesticks, one chafing dish, two Iron Pots, one Skillet, one pair of brass and-Irons, one pair of fire Tongs, one Shovel, one Iron Spitt, one smoothing Iron and Heater, one dozen of silver Spoons, one Silver Porringer, one large Trunk, covered with Russia Leather one

Seal Skin small Trunk marked J. S. C. one Chest that she keeps her Clothes in.

ITEM I Give and Bequeath to my said Wife all her Wearing Apparel both Linen and Woollen of what nature soever they be, and Silks withall her Rings, Jewells, and a Gold chain, or locket —

ITEM I likewise give to my said Wife Sarah Custis twenty four head of Cattle, and twenty two Sheep.

ITEM my Will and desire is, that before my Estate is divided, that all my just Debts and Legacies be paid ; and that is my desire that my executors make no delay to pay them ; All the rest of my Estate I Give and Bequeath unto my loving wife Sarah Custis, Hancock Custis, Henry Custis, Elizabeth Custis, Sorrowful Margaret Kendall to be equally divided amongst them whether they be goods, Chattels, Creatures, Money or Debts, and upon Division if my Wife have a mind of any particular thing to have her first choice. I desire my Good friends Captain William Harmanson, George Harmanson, and M. Hilary Stringer to be aiding and assisting my wife and Children to divide my said Estate, I do nominate and appoint my loving wife Sarah Custis, my son Hancock Custis, my son Henry Custis, to be my executors of this my last will & Testament & I do make void all former Wills by me made and Deeds of Gifts whatsoever.

ITEM I Give and bequeath unto William Harmanson, M. George Harmanson, and M. Hilary Stringer each of them a Gold Ring of the Value of fifteen shillings apiece to be sent for by my executors. I Give to my Sister in law Elishe Frank two Cows and Cafs and as much stuff as will [make] her Gown and Petticoat as much new good Linen as will make her three Shifts.

ITEM I Give all my wearing apparel to my two Sons Hancock Custis and Henry Custis, of what nature soever to be equally divided amongst them by my now Wife.

ITEM I Give to Robert Howsen [1] fifteen Shillings to buy him a Gold ring, to be sent for as aforesaid, and either a young Mare or Horse.

In Testimony that this is my last will & Testament I have here-

---

1 The site of Alexandria was included in a grant of 6000 acres of land fronting the Potomac River, and extending from Hunting Creek to the Little Falls, from Sir William Berkeley, Governor of Virginia, to Robert Howson, in October, 1669. — BROCK.

unto set my hand [and] Seal this third Day of December in the Year of our Lord God, one thousand seven hundred & eight.

Test   ROBERT HOWSEN   JOHN CUSTIS (L S)

JOHN SATCHELL   NORTHAMPTON COUNTY Ss! March the 10th $\frac{1713}{14}$

SARAH S P PALMER   The said Will and Testament of John

Signum
ELISHE FRANK   Custis Esqr was presented to Court by

her mark
ELIZABETH ✕ ATKINSON   his Relict Mrs Sarah Custis, and his two Sons Hancock Custis and Henry Custis his Executors who made Oath thereto, and upon their Motions it is proved in Court by the Oaths of Robert Housen, John Satchell, and Elishe Frank Witnesses thereto is admitted to record, and according to order it is recorded.

Teste ROBERT HOWSON ⎱ C. Cir^t Co^t Northampton
Recorded Teste ROBERT HOUSEN ^{1} ⎰

A Codicil which I Annex to this my last Will & Testament, and I desire that it be truly and punctually performed as any part of my Will whatever.

ITEM that whereas I have in my Will given my now dwelling House and Plantation withall the Appurtenances thereto belonging I mean the use of it to my loving wife Sarah Custis during her natural life, Always provided that if she Marries that her husband immediately enter into Bond with good Security as in my said Will is set forth, Now my desire is that if my said Wife should Marry, and her Husband refuse to give Bond with Secur-
                                                                    then
ity to my said Son Hancock Custis or his heirs ⋀ it shall be law-ful for my said Wife to enjoy her thirds, as the law in such Cases provides.^{2} Whereas I gave a parcel of Land to Yardly Michael

---

1 This name in the copy of the will sent to Washington is spelled Housen, Howsen, and Howson.   The latter is correct.

2 There is a striking contrast in the affectionate manner in which this John Custis provides for the comfort of his wife and the tombstone of his eldest son, on which is the following inscription : —

Beneath this Marble Tomb lies ye body
of the Honorable John Custis, Esq.,
of the City of Williamsburg and Parish of Bruton
Formerly of Hungars Parish on the Eastern Shore of
Virginia and the County of Northampton the
place of his nativity.
Aged 71 years and yet lived but seven years   Which

containing three hundred Acres whereon he formerly lived, I do revoke that Gift, as if it had never been made, and I do give the said Land withall the advantages thereto belonging with one hundred Acres of Land thereto belonging to the sole use and Benefit of my now dwelling Plantation to be used by them that are the true Possessors of this my now dwelling Plantation for Timber or otherwise forever. Whereas I have given five hundred Acres of Land on Jingoteague Island in my Will in common as is there expressed to explain my meaning, my Will and desire is, that my said daughters enjoy the said Land & Negros during their natural lives, and likewise their Husbands, but after their decease, then to go to which Child of their two Bodies lawfully begotten my said two sons in law, and my daughters shall think fit, that is if they are not pleased to give it to the eldest, then to any other which they please, still to be held in common; I mean the Land; but the Negros to be distributed amongst my Grand Children as they shall think fit, and whereas I have given my dear wife liberty of range for twenty head of Cattle, on Pocomock, and Gingoteague Island if she is not pleased to accept of that consideration for her thirds on that Land she may refuse, and then her thirds not to be debared her. this I have Writ with my own hand the more to confirm the same.

Teste   JOHN CUSTIS - - - (L S)

ROBERT HOWSEN
MATTHEW NEWMAN   And my desire is, and I will
SARAH CUSTIS ✕ MATTHEWS   and bequeath to my dear wife
Signum   all the grain of what sort soever shall be found on my Plantation either in Growing in the field or lying in the Houses together withall my Hogs for her support, and my Will and desire is that the Smith Tools I shall be or am Possessed with shall go, and I give them to my daughter Elizabeth Custis, and her heirs forever, and my Will is, that the Male Cattle given to my son John Custis in my Will bars him

---

Which was the space of time he kept
A Bachelor's House at Arlington
On the Eastern Shore of Virginia.
This information put on this tomb was by his
own positive order.

of any further claim, I owed him of nineteen head, and I owed him for the exchange of his part of Pocomock being I am sensisible many more ; and my Will and desire is ; that my Girl Abigail that I formerly gave to my daughter Margaret in my Will be and remain withall her increase to my Grandson Custis Kendall and his heirs and Assigns forever: Whereas I am sensible of my interlinings in my Will all that can be thought of my Writing or M.r Howsons I do confirm, and desire that_∧ this part of my Codicil with the rest may be perpetually performed Signed, Sealed and Acknowledged as the part or Codicil Annexed to my Will before JOHN CUSTIS - - (L S)

JOHN ATKINSON ⎫
ELIZABETH FOX ⎬ Witnesses   March the 20.th 17¹¹⁄₁₂
ROBERT HOWSEN ⎭   Upon consideration of a late Act of Assembly made at Williamsburg the last Sessions,[1] my Will and desire is that none of my Estate be appraised as the law set forth, but that my Estate as formerly given in this my Will and Codicil hereto Annexed be divided accordingly, and everyone to enjoy his part in Special. I well hope my Estate will not be in debt, to this I set my hand — the Day and Year above written. The Pistols I design for my son John, I have sent them to him.

JOHN CUSTIS - - (L S)

Signed, Sealed & acknowledged as my ⎫
Act and Deed as a Codicil annexed to ⎪   Nor my executors to
my Will amongst the other Codicils ⎬   give security
before Inserted . . . . ⎭ JOHN CUSTIS – (L. S.)
ROBERT HOWSEN
    Signum
PHILIP P. H. HAMMON   NORTHAMPTON COUNTY, March the 16th 17¹³⁄₁₄
    Signum
WILLIAM N. BANUM   The said three Codicils of John Custis
    Signum
BATT W NOTTINGHAM   Esq.r dec.d being annexed to his said last Will and Testament also presented in Court by his said executors with the said Will, and upon their Motions the said three Codicils was likewise proved in Court by the Oaths of Robert Howsen, Sarah

---

should dye without issue of their Bodyes Lawfully begotten or before they arrive to the Age of twenty one years that then all the aforementioned lands I give to that Son that is Living & if it please god that they should all dye without Issue of their bodyes Lawfully begotten or before they arrive to the age of twenty one years or if I have no more Issue that then I give to my wife those two tracts of Land that Lyes in Stafford County to her and her heirs for Ever the three other tracts to bee divided between what Children It may please god to send my brother if he have but one I give it to him or her if more the Eldest Son to have his Choice of the tracts the next Eldest his next Choice if two Sons, if it be a Daughter that she have her Choice after her brother them & their heirs for ever   ITEM   It is my will that all my ῬsonꝈ Estate in Generall be Equally divided into five parts and that my wife have her first Choice & my Son Lawrence the next my Son John the next my Son NathꝈ the Next & my Son Henry the other   ITEM   it is my will that if [it] please God any of my Sons should dye without Issue of their bodyes Lawfully begotten or before they arrive to the age of Twenty one years that then his part of the Ῥsonall Estate be divided between my wife & the other three Sons Living & if it please God that three of my Sons should dye without issue of their bodyes Lawfully begotten or before they arrive at the age of twenty one years that then the Ῥs.onall Estate be Equally divided between my Wife and that Son that is Living, and if [it] please God that if all my Sᵈ Sons should die without Issue of their bodyes Lawfully begotten or before they arrive at the age of twenty one years that then my Ῥrsonall Estate be Divided Equally between My wife Ann Washington & my brothers Children   ITEM   it is my will that my brother [some words appear to be left out] & tuition of my Son Lawʳ Washington & that my Sᵈ Brother have the keeping of my Sᵈ Sons Estate &c of this my Last [will] & Testamᵗ I make & ordain my well beloved brother Capᵗ Lawrence Washington & my Loving wife Ann Washington my full & whole Excʳ & Executrix.   and I do hereby utterly Disallow revoke & Annull all & Every other former Testamᵗ Wills Legacies bequests & Exˢ by me in any wise before this time named willed & bequested ratifying & Confirming this & none other to be my last will & Testamᵗ   In Witness whereof I have hereunto Set my hand & Seal this day & year as afores'd

Signd Seald publishd Pronounced & declared by the S^d John Washington as his Last Will & Testament in the ꝑrsence of ITEM it is also my will that Mrs Elizabeth Hardid [mutilated] have my Watch that was given to me by Capt Wm Hardidg's Will

ITEM it is my will that my well beloved godson John Du_∧lstone have a gold Signet which was given me by his father on his death bed ITEM it is my Will that my well beloved brother Capt Law^e Washington have my Wearing Rings

JOHN WASHINGTON   [Seal]

JOHN SCOTT   A WEBSTER   THO^S HOWES   PETER HYATT Westmld

At a Court held for the 2^d County the 23rd day of ffeb^ry 1697

The above will was Duly proved & a probat thereof granted the Exec^rs therein Named And Ordered to be recorded

ꝑ^r Cur

Recordat ⸮ 5 May 1697

P^r JA: WESTCOMB Cle Com p^b

Copy Test GEORGE LEE C Ct —

WILL OF MARTHA HAYWARD.[1]

IN THE NAME OF GOD AMEN — I Martha Hayward of the County of Stafford being Sick & weak of body but_∧^of fit Sense & memory thanks be_∧^given to God therefore Doe make & ordaine this my last will & testament.

—

Impr^s I give and bequeath my Soul to God and my body to the Earth to be buryed in Christianlike and Decent manner att the discrestion of my Exe^r hereafter named and as for what wordly Estate it hath pleased God to bless me wth all I give devise and

---

1 Martha Hayward was presumably the daughter of the sister to whom Colonel John Washington the emigrant, in his will, leaves "ten pound out of ye mony I have in England for transporteing herselfe into this Country." Martha Washington married Samuel Hayward, clerk of Stafford County, and brother of Nicholas Hayward, of London.

dispose of in the following manner & forme Item I give and bequeath unto my two Couzins John & Augustine the Sons of my Coz.ⁿ Lawrence Washington of Westmorland County one negroe Woman named Anne and her future increase and in Case of their deaths before they Come to age then I give the Sd negroe to the aforesd Lawrence Washington & his heirs for Ever —

Item I ^give^ unto my Cozen Lawrence Washington Son of M.ʳ John Washington of Westmorland County one mullatto Girl named Suka to him and his heirs for Ever —

Item I give and bequeath unto my Cozen John Washington son of the S.ᵗ John Washington of Westmorland County one mulatto Girl named Kate to him and his heirs for Ever —

Item I give and bequeath my Coz.ⁿ Nathaniell Washington son of the S.ᵈ John Washington one negroe boy named John to him & his heirs for Ever

Item I give and bequeath unto my Coz.ⁿ Hen: Washington Son of the Said John Washington one negroe boy named George William to him and his heirs for Ever —

Item I give and bequeath unto my Kinsman M.ʳ John Washington of Stafford County one negroe Woman named Betty and her future Increase to ^him^ & his heirs for Ever —

Item I give and bequeath unto my Kinsman M.ʳ Rich.ᵈ ffoot two thousand ~~pds~~ Tobbacco to him & his heirs for Ever

Item it is my will and desire that my Exe.ʳ & w.ᵗʰ all Convent Speed after my decease Doe procure and purchase for Each of my Two Sisters in Law viz.ᵗ Mary Wing & Sarah Todd a Servant man or Woman as they or Either [of] them Shall both like haveing att least four or five years to Serve viz.ᵗ I doe give to them and their heirs for Ever —

Item I give and bequeath to my ~~aforesd~~ Six Cozens the Sons of my two Coz.ˢ Lawrence & John Washington of Westmorland County Each of them a feather bedd and furniture to them and their heirs for Ever —

Item it is my will and desire that my Exe.ʳˢ with all Conven.ⁱᵉⁿᶜᵉ Send to England to my [word obliterated] Sister M.ʳˢ Elizabeth Rumbold a Tonn of good Weight of Tobbacco and the Same I give to her and her heirs forever —

Item it is my desire that my Said Execut.rs doe likewise take freight and Send for England to my other Sister M.rs Marg.t Galbut a Tonn of good Weight of Tobbacco which I give to her and her heirs for Ever —

Item I give and bequeath unto M.r W.m Buckner of the County of York a gold Signet —

Item I give and bequeath unto Cap.t Law. Washington and his wife M.r John Washington of Stafford County and his Wife M.r John Washington of Westmorland County and his wife, Mary and Miss Sarah Todd and Mary Wheatly Each of them a gold [ring?] of twenty Shillings price to be procured with all Conven.t Speed after my decease —

Item I give and bequeath unto Sam.ll Todd Son of W.m Todd a heiffer about three years old —

Lastly after all my just Debts are p.d all the rest of my Estate whatsoever and whosesoever I doe give and bequeath unto Cap.t Lawrence Washington M.r John Washington of Westmorland County & M.r John Washington of Stafford County to be Equall divided between them and doe hereby [word obliterated] Constitute and ordaine the ~~aforesd~~ Lawrence Washington of Westmorland ~~County Execut.rs~~ & John Washington of Westmorland County Execut.rs of this my last Will & Testament   In Witnesse whereof I have hereunto Set my hand & fixed my Seale this 6.th day of May Anno Domi 1697/ Martha Hayward [Seale]

Signd Sealed and Delivered In the presence of us Geo. Weedon Sarah Kelly Sarah ∞ Powell her marke John Pike

Proved and Recorded the 8.th December 1697/

Vera Copia Test

W. Parry.   D Co Cur Com. Stafford

WILL OF LAWRENCE WASHINGTON.[1]

In the name of God Amen I Lawrence Washington of Washington parish in the County of Westmo[re]land in Virginia gentle-

---

[1] Grandfather of George.

man being of good and perfect memory thanks be unto almighty God for it and calling to mind the uncertane Estate of this transitory Life and that all flesh must yeild unto death when it shall please God for to call doe make constitute ordaind and declare this my last will and Testament in manner and form following, revoking and annulling by these presents all and every Testament and Testaments will or wills heartofore by me made and declared either by word or writing and this to be taken only for my Last will and Testament and no other. and first being heartily sorry from the bottom of my heart for my Sines most humbly deserving [1] forgiveness of the same from the allmighty God my saviour and Redeemer in whom by the merits of Jesus Christ I trust and beleive assuredly to be saved and to have full remission and forgiveness of all my Sines, and that my — Soule with my body at the general day of resurrection shall rise againe with joy and through the merits of Christs death and passion possess and inherit the Kingdom of heaven prepared for his Elect and chosen, and my body to be buryed if please God I Depart in this County of Westmorland by the side of my father and mother & neare my Brother and Sister & my Children. and now for the setling of my temporal Estate and such goods Chattells & debts & it hath pleased God farr above my deserts to bestow upon me I doe ordaine give and dispose the same in manner & form following In primis. I will that all those Debts and dues that I owe in right or conseince to any manner of person or persons whatsoever shall be well Contented & paid ordained to be paid by my Executor or Executrix hereafter named. Item I give and bequeath to my well beloved friends Mr William Thompson Clerk Mr Samuel Thompson each of them a mourning ring of thirty Shillings price each Ring. Item I give and bequeath to my Godson Lawrence Butler one young mare & two cowes. Item I give and bequeath to my sister Ann Writts Children one man Servant a piece of four or five years to Serve or three thousand pounds of Tobacco to purchase the same to be delivered or paid to them when they arrive to the age of twenty years old. Item I give and bequeath to my Sister Lewis a mourning ring of forty Shillings price. Item I give my

---

[1] So in manuscript.

Cozen John Washington Sen.r of Stafford-County all my wereing apparell. Item I give unto my Cozen John Washington eldest son Lawrence Washington my Godson one man Servent of four or five yeares to serve, or three thousand pounds of Tobacco to purchase the same to be paid him when he comes to the age of twenty years old. Item I give to my Godson[s] Lawrence Butler and Lewis Nicholas — that tract of Land joyning upon Meridah Edwards and Danil White being two hundred and Seventy five acres to be equally divided between them and their heirs for ever. Item I give to the upper and Lower Churches of Washington parish each of them a pulpit Cloath and Cushing. Item it is my will to have a funerall Sermon at the Church & to have now other funerall to exceed three thousand pounds of Tobacco. Item it is my will after my debts & Legacies are paid that my personall Estate be equally divided in to four parts my Loving wife Mildred Washington to have one part my Son John Washington to have another part my Son Augustine Washington to have another part & my daughter Mildred Washington to have the other part. (to be paid and delivered to them in Specie when they shall come to the age of twenty years old) Item I give to my Son John Washington this seat of Land where I now Live and that whole tract of Land Lying from the mouth of Machotick extending to [a] place called the round hill with the addition I have thereunto made of William Webb and William Rush to him and his Heires for ever. Item I give a[nd] bequeath unto my Son Augustine Washington all the dividend of Land that I bought of M.r Robert Lissons Children in England, Lying in Mattox between my Brother and M.r Baldridges Land Where M.r Daniel Lisson formerly lived by estimation four hundred Acres to him and his heires for Ever, as likewise that Land that was M.r Richard Hills. Item I give & bequeath unto my Said Son Augustine Washington all that tract of Land where M.r Lewis Markham now Lives after the said Markhams and his now wives [1] decease by estimation Seven hundred acres more or less to him and his heirs for Ever Item I give and bequeath my daughter Mildred Washington all my Land in Stafford County — Lying upon Hunting Creek where M.rs Eliz.a Minton and M.rs Williams now Lives by estimation two

---

1 So in manuscript.

thousand five hundred acres, to her and her heires for Ever.[1]
Item it is my will and desire if either of my Children should
die before they come of age or day of marriage, his or her personal Estate be equally divided between the two Survivors and
their mother. Item it is my will and desire if all my Children
should die before they come of age or day of Marriage that my
brothers Children shall enjoy all their estate, excepting that Land
that I bought of Mr Robert Lissons Children which I give to
my Loving wife and her heires for ever, and the rest as afore
said to them and their heirs for ever. Item I give my personal
estate in case of all my Childrens death as aforesaid to be equally
divided between my wife and Brothers Children my wife to
have the one halfe. Item I give that Land which I bought of
my Brother [blank] Wright being two hundred acres Lying near
Markhams[2] Quarter to my Son John Washington and his heirs
for Ever. Item it is my desire that my Estate should not be
appraised but kept intire, and delivered them as above given
according to him[8] and my Children to continue under the care
and tuition of their mother till they come of age or day of marriage and she to have the profits of their estates towards the
bringing of them up and Keeping them to School. Item I doe
ordaine and appoint my Cozen John Washington of Stafford
County and my Friend Mr Samuel Thompson my Executors and
my Loving wife Mildred Washington my Executrix, of this my
last will and Testament. In witness whereof I have hereunto Set
my hand and Seal this 11th day of March Anno Domini 169⅞
LAWRENCE WASHINGTON [Seal] Sign'd Seald declared and pronounced in presence of ROBERT REDDMAN GEORGE WEEDON
THOMAS HOWES JOHN ROSIER.

Witness At a Court held for the said County the 30th day of
March 1698.

The last will and Testament of Lawrence Washington gentleman dec'd within writing was proved by the oaths of George
Weedon Thomas Howes and John Rosier three of the witness's

---

[1] There appears here in this will as given in Ford's *Washington Wills*, "Item
I give my water mill to my son John Washington to him and his heirs forever." This
item is not in the copy found in the manuscripts.

[2] In Ford's *Washington Wills* this reads "Storkes."

[8] So in manuscript; should read "time."

thereto subscribed A Probat thereof granted to Samuel Thompson gentl one of the Executors therein named, and the will ordered to be Recorded P.r Cur.

Ja : Westcomb Cla Com pb

Recordat tertio die April 1698 Eundm Chum

Cop:ᵃ Eai P.r Thomas Borrell

WILL OF AUGUSTINE WASHINGTON.[1]

In the Name of God Amen

I Augustine Washington of the County of King George Gent:
being sick and ∧ but of Perfect and Disposing Sence and Memory
^{weak}

do make my Last will and Testament in Manner following her ∧ by
Revoking all former will or wills whatsoever by me hertofore made

Imprimis I Give unto my Son Lawrence Washington & his Heirs for ever All that Plantation and Tract of Land at Hunting Creek in the County of Prince William Containing by Estimation Two Thous : five Hundred Acres with the water mill Adjoining thereto or Lying Near the same, and all the Slaves Cattle and Stocks of all Kinds whatsoever ∧ all the Houshold Furniture Whatsoever now in and upon or w.ch have been Commonly Poses,d by my said son together with the Said Plantation Tract of Land and mill . . . .

Item I give Unto my son Augustine Washington and his Heirs for Ever all my Lands in the County of Westmorland Except such only as are herein after otherwise Disposed of. Together with Twenty five Head of Neat Cattle, forty Hogs and Twenty Sheep and a Negro Man named Fra[n]k besides those Negro,s formerly Given him by his Mother . . . .

Item I Give unto my said son Augustine three Young Working Slaves to be purchased for him out of the first Profits of the Iron Works [2] after my Decease . . . .

---

1 Father of George Washington.

2 For a full description of the Principio Company (manufacturers of pig and bar iron in Maryland and Virginia), in which Augustine Washington owned a one twelfth share, see *Pennsylvania Magazine of History and Biography*, 1887.

ITEM I give Unto my son George Washington and his Heirs the Land I now Live on which I Purchased of the Executrix of Mr William Strother Deceased, and one Moiety of my Land Lying on Deep Run and [blank] Negro Slaves. . . . .

ITEM I give Unto my son Samuel Washington & his Heirs my Land at Chotank in the County of Stafford Containing about Six Hundred Acres and Also the other Moiety of my Tract of Land Lying on Deep Run . . . .

ITEM I give unto my ^Son John Washington and his Heirs my Land at the Head of Maddox in the County of Westmorland Containing About Seven Hundred Acres. . . . .

ITEM I give unto my Son Charles Washington and his Heirs the Land I Purchased of my son Lawrence Washington (whereon Thomas Lewis now Lives) Adjoyning to my said son Lawrence,s Land Above Devised, I also give Unto my ^said son Charles and his Heirs the Land I Purchased of Gabril Adams, in the County of Prince William, Containing about Seven Hundred Acres . . .

ITEM it is my will and Desire that all the Rest of my Negro,s not herein Particularly Devised may be Equally Divided between my Wife and my three sons Samuel John & Charles and that Ned Jack Bob Sue & Lucy may be Included in my Wifes part which part of my said Wifes after her Decease I Desire may be Equally Divided between my sons George Samuel John & Charles and the part of my said Negroes so Divided [1] to my Wife I mean and Intend to be in full Satisfaction & Lieu of her Dower in my Negro,s but ^if she should Insist Notwithstanding ^on her Right of Dower in my Negroes I will and Desire that so many as may be Wanting to make up her share may be Taken out of the Negroes Given hereby to my sons George Samuel John & Charles . . .

ITEM I give and Bequ ^eath Unto my said Wife and four sons George Samuel John & Charles all the Rest of my Personall Estate to be Equally Divided Between them which is not Particu-larly Bequeath'd By this my Will And it is my Will ^& Desire that my said four Sons Estates may be Kept in my Wifes hands untill the[y] Respectively Attain the Age of twenty one years in Case my

---

[1] So in manuscript; should read "devised."

Said Wife Continues so Long Unmarried but in Case She Should happen to marry before that time I desire it may be In the power of my Executors to oblige her Husband from time to time as they shall think proper to give Security for the performance of this my Last will in paying & Delivering my said four sons their Estates Respectively as they come of age or on failure to give such Security to take my said sons & their Estates out of the Custody & Tuition of my ^{sd}∧wife & her Husband. . . . .

ITEM I give and Bequeath unto my said wife the Crops made at Bridge Creek Chotank and Rappahannock quarters at the time of my Decease for the Suport of her Self and her Childred & I Desire my Wife may Have the Liberty of working my Land at Bridge Creek quarter for the term of five Years Next after my Decease during wch time She may fix a quarter on deep Run . .

ITEM I give to my son Lawrence Washington and the Heirs of his body Lawfully Begotten for Ever that Tract of ∧^{land} I purchased of Mr James How [1] Adjoyning to the said Lawrence Washingtons Land on Mattox in the County of Westmorland wch I give him in lieu of the Land my Said son bought for me in Prince William County of Spence & Harrison & for want of such Heirs then I give & desire [2] the Land to my Son Augustine and his Heirs for Ever . . . .

ITEM I give to my said son Lawrence all the Right title & Interest I have to in or out of the Iron Works in which I am Concer[n]d in Virginia and Maryland Provided that he do & shall out of the profits Raised thereby Purchase for my son Augustine three young Working Slaves as have herein Before Directed and Also pay my Daughter Betty When she Arives to the age of Eighteen Years the sum of four Hundred pounds which Right Title and Interest on the Condition Aforesaid I give to my said son Lawrence and his Heirs for Ever . . . . . .

ITEM I give Unto my said daughter Betty a Negro Child named Mary Daughter to Sue & Another Named Betty daughter to Judy . . . .

ITEM It is my will & desire that my sons Lawrence and Au-

---

[1] Ford, in the *Washington Wills*, prints this name as " Nore," but in the copy preserved among the Washington Papers it is written " How."

[2] So in manuscript ; should read " devise."

gustine do pay out of the Respective Estate Devis.d to them one half or Moiety of the Debts I justly owe & for that purpose I give_∧to my two sons one half of the Debts due and owing to
^{and bequeath}
me . . . .

ITEM forasmuch as my Severall Children in this my Will Mentioned being by Severall Ventors Cannot Inherit from one Another in Order to make proper provission against their Dying Without Issue It is my will & Desire that in Case my Son Lawrence Should die without Heirs of his Body Lawfully Begotten that then the Land & mill Given him by this my Will Lying in the County of Prince William Shall go and Remain to my son George & his Heirs but In Case my son Augustine should Chose to have the Said Land Rather than the Land she holds in Mattox Either by this wlll or any Settlement then I give and Desire the Said Lands in Pri[n]ce William to my Said Son Augustine and his Heirs on his Conveying the Said Lands in Mattox to my said son George and his Heirs and in Case my said son Augustine Shall happen to dye w.[out] Issue of his Body Lawfully Begotten then I Give and Bequeath all the said Lands by him held in Mattox to my said son George and his Heirs and_∧both my sons Lawrence and Augustine should happen to dye without Issue of their Severall Bodys Begotten then my Will and Desire is that my son George and his Heirs may have his and their Choice to have Either the Lands of my_∧Augustine to hold to him and his Heirs and the Lands of such_∧my said sons Lawrence or Augustine as Shall not be_∧chosen by my son George and or his Heirs Shall go to and Be Equally Divided among my sons Samuel John & Charles and their Heirs Share & Share Alike and in Case my son George by the Death of both or Either of my Sons Lawrence and Augustine Should According to this my Intention come to Be posses'd of either_∧Lands then my will and Desire is that the Lands hereby Devis,d to my said son George and his Heirs Shall Go Over and be Equally Divided Betwe_∧n my sons Samuel & John and their Heirs Share & Share Alike

and in Case all my Children by my present Wife Should happen
to dye without Issue of their Bodys Then my will and Desire is
that all the Lands by this my will Devised to any of my said Children should go to my sons Augustine & Lawrence if Living and
to their Heirs if one of them Should be Dead w^{th}out Issue
then to the Survivor and his Heirs but my True Intins and
Mea[n]ing is that Each of my Children by my Present Wife may
have their Lands in fee Simple Upon the Contingency of their
Arriving at full Age or Leaving Heirs of their Bodys Lawfully
Begotten or on their dying Under Age and without Lawfull Issue
their Severall parts to Desend from one to a Nother According to
their Coars of Desents and the Remainder over of the[i]r or any
of their Land in this Claws mentioned to my sons Lawrence &
Augustine or the Survivor of them is only Upon the Contingency
of all my Said Children by my present wife dying under Age &
without Issue Living my sons Lawrence and Augustine or Either
of them . . . .

LASTLY I constitute and Appoint my son Lawrence Washington
and my good Friends Danniel Mc Carty and Nathaniel Chapman
Gen^t Executors of this my Last will and Testament In Witness
Whereof I have hereunto sett my Hand & Seal the Eleventh day
Aprill 1743.

Sign,d Seald, and Publish,d   AUGUSTINE WASHINGTON
in the presence of us
   ROB^T. JACKSON
   ANTHONY STROTHER
   JAMES THOMSON

Provided further that if my Land in Chotank Devised to my Son
Samuel should by Course of Law be taken away[1] then I give to

---

[1] There is in Hening, vol vi. p. 513, "An Act to confirm and establish an agreement
made between William Withers and Augustine Washington" relative to "a certain tract
or parcel of land, lying and being in the parish of St. Paul, in the county of Stafford,
containing five hundred and thirty three acres, more or less, called and known by the
name of Chotank." William Withers had a claim upon the land through the will of
John Withers (August 9, 1698), who devised it to his daughter Sarah, and after her
death to his cousin William Withers and heirs male; but in default of such issue to
Thomas Withers and his heirs male; or in want of such heirs "to any one proving
themselves of the name of Withers." William Withers died without issue; Thomas
died in England leaving a son Edmund his heir. William, brother of Edmund, inherited from him, who died leaving male issue, Thomas, after whose death the title was

The Riverside Press

Electrotyped and printed by H. O. Houghton & Co.
Cambridge, Mass., U. S. A.

to Washington